THE PRINCE

Niccolò Machiavelli

SPARK PUBLISHING

SPARKNOTES is a registered trademark of SparkNotes LLC

Spark Publishing
A Division of Barnes & Noble
120 Fifth Avenue
New York, NY 10011
www.sparknotes.com

ISBN-13: 978-1-4114-0714-5
ISBN-10: 1-4114-0714-8

Please submit changes or report errors to www.sparknotes.com/errors.

Printed in the United States

10 9 8 7 6 5 4 3 2

Contents

Context

Biographical and Historical Background

Niccolò Machiavelli was born on May 3, 1469, in Florence, Italy, and passed his childhood peacefully, receiving the humanistic education customary for young men of the Renaissance middle class. He also spent two years studying business mathematics, then worked for the next seven years in Rome for a Florentine banker. After returning to Florence in 1494, he witnessed the expulsion of the Medici family, oligarchic despots who had ruled Florence for decades, and the rise of Girolamo Savanorola, a Dominican religious zealot who took control of the region shortly thereafter.

Italy at that time became the scene of intense political conflict. The city-states of Florence, Milan, Venice, and Naples fought for control of Italy, as did the papacy, France, Spain, and the Holy Roman Empire. Each of these powers attempted to pursue a strategy of playing the other powers off of one other, but they also engaged in less honorable practices such as blackmail and violence. The same year that Machiavelli returned to Florence, Italy was invaded by Charles VIII of France—the first of several French invasions that would occur during Machiavelli's lifetime. These events influenced Machiavelli's attitudes toward government, forming the backdrop for his later impassioned pleas for Italian unity.

Because Savanorola criticized the leadership of the Church, Pope Alexander VI cut his reign short by excommunicating him in 1497. The next year, at the age of twenty-nine, Machiavelli entered the Florentine government as head of the Second Chancery and secretary to the Council of Ten for War. In his role as chancellor, he was sent to France on a diplomatic mission in 1500. He met regularly with Pope Alexander and the recently crowned King Louis XII. In exchange for a marriage annulment, Louis helped the pope establish his son, Cesare Borgia, as the duke of Romagna. The intrigues of these three men would influence Machiavelli's political thought, but it was Borgia who would do the most to shape Machiavelli's opinions about leadership. Borgia was a cunning, cruel, and vicious politician, and many people despised him. Nevertheless, Machiavelli believed Borgia had the traits necessary for any leader who would seek to unify Italy.

In 1500, Machiavelli married Marietta di Lodovico Corsini, with whom he had six children. Three years later, Pope Alexander VI became sick with malaria and died. Alexander VI's successor died after less than a month in office, and Julius II, an enemy of Borgia's, was elected. Julius II later banished Borgia to Spain, where he died in 1506.

Meanwhile, Machiavelli helped raise and train a Florentine civil militia in order to reduce Florence's dependence on mercenaries. Later that year, he served as Florentine diplomat to Pope Julius, whose conduct as the "warrior pope" he observed firsthand. In 1512, the Medici family regained control of Florence, and Machiavelli was dismissed from office. A year later he was wrongly accused of participating in a conspiracy to restore the republic, held in jail for three weeks, and tortured on the rack. He left Florence for the quiet town of Sant'Andrea and decided to pursue a career in writing. In 1513 he began writing his *Discourses on the First Ten Books of Titus Livius,* a book that focused on states controlled by a politically active citizenry. It was not finished until 1521, mainly because he interrupted his work on *Discourses* to write *The Prince.*

Machiavelli desperately wanted to return to politics. One of his goals in writing *The Prince* was to win the favor of Lorenzo de' Medici, then-governor of Florence and the person to whom the book is dedicated; Machiavelli hoped to land an advisory position within the Florentine government. But Medici received the book indifferently, and Machiavelli did not receive an invitation to serve as an official. The public's reaction to *The Prince* was also indifferent at first. But slowly, as word spread, the book began to be criticized as immoral, evil, and wicked.

Besides the *Discourses,* Machiavelli went on to write *The Art of War* and a comedic play, *The Mandrake.* After Lorenzo's premature death in 1519, his successor, Giulio, gave Machiavelli a commission to write *The Florentine History* as well as a few small diplomatic jobs. Machiavelli also wrote *The Life of Castruccio Castracani* in 1520 and *Clizia,* a comedic play. In 1526, Giulio de' Medici (now Pope Clement VII), at Machiavelli's urging, created a commission to examine Florence's fortifications and placed Machiavelli on it.

In 1527, the diplomatic errors of the Medici pope resulted in the sack of Rome by Charles V's mercenaries. The Florentines expelled their Medici ruler, and Machiavelli tried to retake the office he had left so before. But his reputation got in the way of his ambitions. He was now too closely associated with the Medicis, and the republic rejected him. Soon, Machiavelli's health began to fail him, and he died several months later, on June 21, 1527.

Philosophical Context

> [A]nyone compelled to choose will find greater security in being feared than in being loved.
>
> (See QUOTATIONS, p. 44)

The most revolutionary aspect of *The Prince* is its separation of politics and ethics. Classical political theory traditionally linked political law with a higher, moral law. In contrast, Machiavelli argues that political action must always be considered in light of its practical consequences rather than some lofty ideal.

Another striking feature of *The Prince* is that it is far less theoretical than the literature on political theory that preceded it. Many earlier thinkers had constructed hypothetical notions of ideal or natural states, but Machiavelli treated historical evidence pragmatically to ground *The Prince* in real situations. The book is dedicated to the current ruler of Florence, and it is readily apparent that Machiavelli intends for his advice to be taken seriously by the powerful men of his time. It is a practical guide for a ruler rather than an abstract treatise of philosophy.

Machiavelli's book also distinguishes itself on the subject of free will. Medieval and Renaissance thinkers often looked to religion or ancient authors for explanations of plagues, famines, invasions, and other calamities; they considered the actual prevention of such disasters to be beyond the scope of human power. In *The Prince,* when Machiavelli argues that people have the ability to shield themselves against misfortune, he expresses an extraordinary confidence in the power of human self-determination and affirms his belief in free will as opposed to divine destiny.

Since they were first published, Machiavelli's ideas have been oversimplified and vilified. His political thought is usually—and unfairly—defined solely in terms of *The Prince.* The adjective "Machiavellian" is used to mean "manipulative," "deceptive," or "ruthless." But Machiavelli's *Discourses*, a work considerably longer and more developed than *The Prince,* expounds republican themes of patriotism, civic virtue, and open political participation.

OVERVIEW

MACHIAVELLI COMPOSED *The Prince* as a practical guide for ruling. This goal is evident from the very beginning, the dedication of the book to Lorenzo de' Medici, the ruler of Florence. *The Prince* is not particularly theoretical or abstract; its prose is simple and its logic straightforward. These traits underscore Machiavelli's desire to provide practical, easily understandable advice.

The first two chapters describe the book's scope. *The Prince* is concerned with autocratic regimes, not with republican regimes. The first chapter defines the various types of principalities and princes; in doing so, it constructs an outline for the rest of the book. Chapter III comprehensively describes how to maintain composite principalities—that is, principalities that are newly created or annexed from another power, so that the prince is not familiar to the people he rules. Chapter III also introduces the book's main concerns—power politics, warcraft, and popular goodwill—in an encapsulated form.

Chapters IV through XIV constitute the heart of the book. Machiavelli offers practical advice on a variety of matters, including the advantages and disadvantages that attend various routes to power, how to acquire and hold new states, how to deal with internal insurrection, how to make alliances, and how to maintain a strong military. Implicit in these chapters are Machiavelli's views regarding free will, human nature, and ethics, but these ideas do not manifest themselves explicitly as topics of discussion until later.

Chapters XV to XXIII focus on the qualities of the prince himself. Broadly speaking, this discussion is guided by Machiavelli's underlying view that lofty ideals translate into bad government. This premise is especially true with respect to personal virtue. Certain virtues may be admired for their own sake, but for a prince to act in accordance with virtue is often detrimental to the state. Similarly, certain vices may be frowned upon, but vicious actions are sometimes indispensable to the good of the state. Machiavelli combines this line of reasoning with another: the theme that obtaining the goodwill of the populace is the best way to maintain power. Thus, the *appearance* of virtue may be more important than true virtue, which may be seen as a liability.

The final sections of *The Prince* link the book to a specific historical context: Italy's disunity. Machiavelli sets down his account and explanation of the failure of past Italian rulers and concludes with an impassioned plea to the future rulers of the nation. Machiavelli asserts the belief that only Lorenzo de' Medici, to whom the book is dedicated, can restore Italy's honor and pride.

Terms & People

Agathocles Ruler of Syracuse (317–310 B.C.) who conquered all of Sicily except for territory dominated by Carthage; he was eventually defeated by the Carthaginian army.

Alexander Alexander the Great, king of Macedonia (336–323 B.C.). He conquered Greece, Persia, and much of Asia.

Alexander VI Elected pope in 1492. Challenged by French invasion of Italy and a war between France and Spain. Father of Cesare Borgia.

Auxiliary troops Troops borrowed from other nations to fight for a prince. Organized and effective in battle, they nonetheless have loyalties to their home state.

Cesare Borgia Also called Duke Valentino (1476–1507). Cesare Borgia was made duke of Romagna by his father, Pope Alexander VI, in 1501. He lost power after the death of the pope. Cesare Borgia is Machiavelli's primary example of a prince who has great prowess, as displayed by his efforts to secure his state quickly after he was put in power.

Composite principality A principality that is either newly created or annexed from another power. These principalities can differ in their culture, language, and attitudes in relation to the prince, since he is an unfamiliar ruler. These principalities pose the most difficulties.

Cyrus Founder of the Persian Empire.

Ecclesiastical principalities A principality technically under the rulership of a prince, but nonetheless strongly dominated by the Church.

TERMS & PEOPLE

Hereditary principality A principality ruled by a prince whose family has controlled the principality for several generations. Hereditary principalities, according to Machiavelli, are generally easy to rule and maintain.

Julius II Reigned as pope 1503–1513. Julius II strengthened the power of the Church through vigorous leadership and intelligent diplomacy. He defeated Roman barons and negotiated an alliance against France.

Leo X Elected pope in 1513. Leo X was an advocate of the Medici family.

Mercenary troops Troops that are paid to perform a service for the prince. Because they have no loyalty to the prince, and money is their only inducement to fight, they are unreliable as a means of defense. They will be unwilling to die in battle and therefore will not fight vigorously.

Native troops Broad term to describe the native army of a principality, consisting of countrymen and commanded either by a prince himself or a confidant.

Principality A localized territory or region ruled by a prince (or princess), from which the term is derived. A prince may rule more than one principality. All principalities can be grouped under the general category of "state." A principality is ruled autocratically and is therefore distinguished from a republic, the only other type of state. For the most part, the advice found in *The Prince* is geared toward principalities, although the book does reference republics in some cases.

Prowess The ability to conquer and govern. Machiavelli uses this term as the opposite of "fortune."

Republic   A state not ruled by a monarch or prince but headed by elected officials accountable to a larger citizenry. Machiavelli distinguishes a republic from a principality, which the bulk of *The Prince* takes as its subject.

Romulus   Founder and first king of Rome.

Septimius Severus Roman emperor (A.D. 193–211).

Theseus   Hero of Attica, king of Athens. According to legend, he killed the Minotaur in the Cretan labyrinth.

TERMS & PEOPLE

THEMES

STATESMANSHIP & WARCRAFT

Machiavelli believes that good laws follow naturally from a good military. His famous statement that "the presence of sound military forces indicates the presence of sound laws" describes the relationship between developing states and war in *The Prince*. Machiavelli reverses the conventional understanding of war as a necessary, but not definitive, element of the development of states, and instead asserts that successful war is the very foundation upon which all states are built. Much of *The Prince* is devoted to describing exactly what it means to conduct a good war: how to effectively fortify a city, how to treat subjects in newly acquired territories, and how to prevent domestic insurrection that would distract from a successful war. But Machiavelli's description of war encompasses more than just the direct use of military force—it comprises international diplomacy, domestic politics, tactical strategy, geographic mastery, and historical analysis. Within the context of Machiavelli's Italy—when cities were constantly threatened by neighboring principalities and the area had suffered through power struggles for many years—his method of viewing almost all affairs of state through a military lens was a timely innovation in political thinking.

GOODWILL & HATRED

To remain in power, a prince must avoid the hatred of his people. It is not necessary for him to be loved; in fact, it is often better for him to be feared. Being hated, however, can cause a prince's downfall. This assertion might seem incompatible with Machiavelli's statements on the utility of cruelty, but Machiavelli advocates the use of cruelty only insofar as it does not compromise the long-term goodwill of the people. The people's goodwill is always the best defense against both domestic insurrection and foreign aggression. Machiavelli warns princes against doing things that might result in hatred, such as the confiscation of property or the dissolution of traditional institutions. Even installations that are normally valued for military use, such as fortresses, should be judged primarily on their potential to garner support for the prince. Indeed, only when he is absolutely sure that the people who hate him will never be able to rise against him can a prince cease to worry about incurring the hatred of any of his subjects. Ultimately, however, obtaining the goodwill of the people has little or nothing to do with a desire for the overall happiness of the populace. Rather, goodwill is a political instrument to ensure the stability of the prince's reign.

FREE WILL

Machiavelli often uses the words "prowess" and "fortune" to describe two distinct ways in which a prince can come to power. "Prowess" refers to an individual's talents, while "fortune" implies chance or luck. Part of Machiavelli's aim in writing *The Prince* is to investigate how much of a prince's success or failure is caused by his own free will and how much is determined by nature or the environment in which he lives. Machiavelli applies this question specifically to the failure of past Italian princes. In Chapter XXV, Machiavelli discusses the role of fortune in determining human affairs. He attempts to compromise between free will and determinism by arguing that fortune controls half of human actions and leaves the other half to free will. However, Machiavelli also argues that through foresight—a quality that he champions throughout the book—people can shield themselves against fortune's vicissitudes. Thus, Machiavelli can be described as confident in the power of human beings to shape their destinies to a degree, but equally confident that human control over events is never absolute.

VIRTUE

Machiavelli defines virtues as qualities that are praised by others, such as generosity, compassion, and piety. He argues that a prince should always try to appear virtuous, but that acting virtuously for virtue's sake can prove detrimental to the principality. A prince should not necessarily avoid vices such as cruelty or dishonesty if employing them will benefit the state. Cruelty and other vices should not be pursued for their own sake, just as virtue should not be pursued for its own sake: virtues and vices should be conceived as means to an end. Every action the prince takes must be considered in light of its effect on the state, not in terms of its intrinsic moral value.

THEMES

HUMAN NATURE

> *Love endures by a bond which men, being scoundrels, may break whenever it serves their advantage to do so; but fear is supported by the dread of pain, which is ever present.*
>
> *(See* QUOTATIONS, *p. 46)*

Machiavelli asserts that a number of traits are inherent in human nature. People are generally self-interested, although their affection for others can be won and lost. They are content and happy so long they are not victims of something terrible. They may be trustworthy in prosperous times, but they will quickly turn selfish, deceitful, and profit-driven in times of adversity. People admire honor, generosity, courage, and piety in others, but most of them do not exhibit these virtues themselves. Ambition is commonly found among those who have achieved some power, but most common people are satisfied with the status quo and therefore do not yearn for increased status. People will naturally feel a sense of obligation after receiving a favor or service, and this bond is usually not easily broken. Nevertheless, loyalties are won and lost, and goodwill is never absolute. Such statements about human nature are often offered up as justifications for the book's advice to princes. While Machiavelli backs up his political arguments with concrete historical evidence, his statements about society and human nature sometimes have the character of assumptions rather than observations.

THEMES

Summary & Analysis

Dedication

Summary
Machiavelli's dedication of *The Prince*—with the heading "Niccolò Machiavelli to the Magnificent Lorenzo de' Medici"—is a letter to Lorenzo de' Medici, the nephew of Giovanni de' Medici (Leo X), who made Machiavelli duke of Urbino in 1516. Machiavelli offers his book with customary humility, commenting that it is stylistically simple and unworthy of his audience. Machiavelli describes his book as a summary of his "understanding of the deeds of great men," intended to help Lorenzo de' Medici achieve eminence as a prince.

Analysis
Machiavelli begins by offering a short defense of why he, an ordinary citizen, should know more than rulers about the art of ruling. He uses a metaphor to justify himself: a person standing on a mountain is best positioned to survey the landscape below, and a person standing below is best positioned to survey the mountain. Similarly, writes Machiavelli, "to comprehend fully the nature of people, one must be a prince, and to comprehend fully the nature of princes one must be an ordinary citizen." Implicit in this claim is the idea that the removed perspective of an observer is a more reliable guide than practical experience, and a better means of improving the art of ruling.

The dedication gives the reader an idea of Machiavelli's intended audience. Though the book has a scholarly tone, it is not for fellow scholars. *The Prince* is meant to advise, instruct, and influence the minds of rulers. It was, originally, a kind of practical "how-to" guide for aspiring princes. Only later did *The Prince* become regarded as an important treatise on political philosophy.

CHAPTERS I–IV

SUMMARY — CHAPTER I: THE KINDS OF PRINCIPALITIES AND THE MEANS BY WHICH THEY ARE ACQUIRED

Machiavelli describes the different kinds of states, arguing that all states are either republics or principalities. Principalities can be divided into hereditary principalities and new principalities. New principalities are either completely new or new appendages to existing states. By fortune or strength, a prince can acquire a new principality with his own army or with the arms of others.

SUMMARY — CHAPTER II: HEREDITARY PRINCIPALITIES

Chapter II is the first of three chapters focusing on methods to govern and maintain principalities. Machiavelli dismisses any discussion of republics, explaining that he has "discussed them at length on another occasion"—a reference to Book 1 of his *Discourses*.

Machiavelli notes that it is easier to govern a hereditary state than a new principality for two main reasons. First, those under the rule of such states are familiar with the prince's family and are therefore accustomed to their rule. The natural prince only has to keep past institutions intact, while adapting these institutions to current events. Second, the natural disposition of subjects in a hereditary state is to love the ruling family, unless the prince commits some horrible act against his people. Even if a strong outsider succeeds in conquering a prince's hereditary state, any setback the outsider encounters will allow the prince to reconquer the state.

SUMMARY — CHAPTER III: MIXED PRINCIPALITIES

> *[M]en must be either pampered or annihilated.*
> *(See* QUOTATIONS, *p. 44)*

Machiavelli explains why maintaining a new principality is more difficult than maintaining a hereditary state. In the first place, people will willingly trade one recently arrived ruler for another, hoping that a new ruler will be better than the present one. This expectation of improvement will induce people to take up arms against any relatively unestablished prince. Although the people may quickly realize that their revolt is ineffective, they will still create great disorder. Furthermore, when a prince takes over another prince's domain, he finds himself in a tricky situation with regard to the people who put him in power. He cannot maintain the support of these people because he cannot fulfill all of their expectations that their situation will improve. But he also cannot deal too harshly with them because he is in their debt. Immediately after taking power, the prince is in danger of losing his newly gained principality.

When a prince successfully suppresses a revolt, however, the ruler can easily prevent further revolt by harshly punishing the rebels and decimating his opposition. The ruler can deal more harshly with his subjects in response to the revolt than he would be able to normally.

It is much easier to maintain control over a new principality if the people share the same language and customs as the prince's own country. If this is the case, the prince has to do only two things: destroy the family of the former prince, and maintain the principality's laws and taxes. People will live quietly and peacefully so long as their old ways of life are undisturbed.

New states that have different languages and customs from those of the prince are more difficult to maintain. One of the prince's most effective options is to take up residence in the new state. By living there, the prince can address problems quickly and efficiently. He can prevent the local officials from plundering his territory. The subjects will be in close contact with the prince. Therefore, those who are inclined to be good will have more reason to show their allegiance to the prince and those who are inclined to be bad will have more reason to fear him. Invaders will think twice before attempting to take over the state.

Another effective method of dealing with linguistic and cultural differences is to establish colonies in the new state. It is less expensive to establish colonies than to maintain military occupation, and colonialism only harms inhabitants who pose no threat to the prince because they are scattered and poor. As a general rule, men must be either pampered or crushed. A prince should injure people only if he knows there is no threat of revenge. Setting up military bases throughout the new state will not effectively keep order. Instead, it will upset the people, and these people may turn into hostile enemies capable of causing great harm to the prince's regime.

A prince who has occupied a state in a foreign country should dominate the neighboring states. He should weaken the strong ones and ensure that no other strong foreign power invades a neighboring state. Weaker powers will naturally side with the strongest power as long as they cannot grow strong themselves. The prince must remain master of the whole country to keep control of the state he has conquered.

Princes should always act to solve problems before problems fully manifest themselves. Political disorders are easy to solve if the prince identifies them and acts early. If they are allowed to develop fully, it will be too late.

Men naturally want to acquire more. When they succeed in acquiring more they are always praised, not condemned. But rulers who lack the ability to acquire, yet still try at the cost of their current state, should be condemned.

In order to hold a state, a prince must understand statecraft and warcraft. The two are intertwined. War can be avoided by suppressing disorder. However, one can never escape a war: war can only be postponed to the enemy's advantage.

SUMMARY — CHAPTER IV: WHY ALEXANDER'S SUCCESSORS WERE ABLE TO KEEP POSSESSION OF DARIUS' KINGDOM AFTER ALEXANDER'S DEATH

There are two ways to govern a principality. The first involves a prince and appointed ministers. While the ministers help govern, everyone remains subservient to the prince. The second way involves a prince and nobles. Nobles are not appointed by the prince, but they benefit from their ancient lineage and have subjects of their own. Of both these scenarios, the prince is regarded as being much stronger if he uses ministers, since he is the only ruler in the country.

It is much harder to take over a country if a prince uses ministers, because ministers have little incentive to be corrupted by foreign powers or to turn on their prince. Furthermore, even if they were to turn against the prince, they would not be able to muster support from any subjects because they hold no personal loyalties. It is easier to conquer a country governed with the cooperation of nobles, because finding a discontented noble eager for change is always possible. Moreover, nobles command the loyalty of their own subjects, so a corrupted noble will corrupt the support of his subjects.

Although it is easier to take over a state ruled by nobles, it is much harder to maintain control of that state. In a state ruled by nobles, it is not enough to kill the former ruler's family, because the nobles will still be around to revolt. Holding onto a state with ministers is much easier, because it merely requires killing off the one prince and his family.

Machiavelli asserts that the rules he proposes are consistent with historical evidence, such as Alexander's successful conquest of Asia and the rebellions against the Romans in Spain, France, and Greece.

ANALYSIS — CHAPTERS I–IV

Machiavelli builds his case through a combination of historical examples and methodical argument. The first step in his argument is to establish the terms and categories that he will use to make sense out of the multitude of different political situations that exist in the real world. The clear-cut distinctions Machiavelli makes between different kinds of states—beginning with principalities and republics—are very effective insofar as they enable him to present his ideas clearly and concisely. Whether his categories do justice to the complexity of political history is a different question. Machiavelli creates an impression of directness and practicality by presenting the world in simple, clearly defined terms.

At the same time, Machiavelli does not rely heavily on theory or abstract thought to make his points; these chapters illustrate his reliance on history as the basis for his theory of government. He sets out to answer the question "How best can a ruler maintain control of his state?" His response, a set of empirically verifiable rules and guidelines, is derived from a study of the conquests of the past, especially those of the French, the Romans, and the Greeks.

One important difference between Machiavelli's philosophy and other philosophies of government lies in his description of the ordinary subject. Aristotle's political writings describe a citizenry that is by nature political and very interested in the welfare of the community. Though Aristotle disregards the majority of people who live within the Greek city-state—women and slaves—he considers the free citizens to be the very reason for the state's existence. Machiavelli, on the other hand, sees the ordinary citizen as a piddling, simpleminded creature. Such people will either love or hate their ruler, depending on whether they are harmed or injured, but as long as the prince can maintain control, he need have little concern for their welfare.

Thus, the purpose of government is not the good of the people but the stability of the state and the perpetuation of the established ruler's control. Machiavelli does not concern himself with what goes on inside the state but what occurs externally. A successful prince must always be aware of foreign powers and the threat of invasion. A focus on power diplomacy and warcraft, at the expense of domestic affairs, is a distinctive element of Machiavelli's project.

Finally, the guidelines set forth in *The Prince* have often been characterized as "amoral" because some of Machiavelli's advice—killing off the family of the former ruler, the violent suppression of revolts and insurrections—seems cruel, brutal, and perhaps downright evil. Whereas the ancient Greeks conceived of a close relationship between ethics and politics, Machiavelli seems to separate these disciplines altogether. Nonetheless, to deny that Machiavelli's political theory accommodates any form of morality and ethics would be inaccurate. For example, religion does play a role in Machiavelli's state. Moreover, although Machiavelli does not use the words "ethical" or "moral" as such, later chapters of *The Prince* suggest that rulers have duties or obligations that could be considered ethical or moral.

CHAPTERS V–VII

SUMMARY — CHAPTER V: HOW TO GOVERN CITIES AND PRINCIPALITIES THAT, PRIOR TO BEING OCCUPIED, LIVED UNDER THEIR OWN LAWS

Machiavelli describes three ways to hold states that have been accustomed to living freely under their own laws. The first is to devastate them. The second is for the conqueror to occupy them. The third is to allow the state to maintain its own laws, but to charge taxes and establish an oligarchy to keep the state friendly. The third option is advantageous because the newly imposed oligarchy will work hard to secure the authority of the conquering prince within the conquered state because it owes its existence to the prince and cannot survive without his support. Thus, as long as the goal is not to devastate the other state, it is easiest to rule it through the use of its own citizens.

Complete destruction is the most certain way of securing a state that has been free in the past. A prince who does not take this route places himself in a position to be destroyed himself. No matter how long it has been since the state was acquired, rebellions will always revive the legacy of ancient institutions and notions of former liberty, even if the state has benefited from the prince's rule. This sense of tradition will unify the people against the prince.

On the other hand, cities or provinces that are accustomed to being ruled by a prince are easy to take over once the ruling family has been destroyed. People in such states are accustomed to obedience and do not know how to live in freedom without having someone to rule over them. Therefore, the new prince can win the province and hold onto it more easily.

In republics (or former republics), sentiments of hatred and revenge against the conquering prince will run strong. The memories of ancient liberty never die, so a prince will be better off destroying the republic or personally occupying the conquered state.

SUMMARY — CHAPTER VI: CONCERNING NEW PRINCIPALITIES ACQUIRED BY ONE'S OWN ARMS AND ABILITY

> [P]eople are by nature changeable. It is easy to persuade them about some particular matter, but it is hard to hold them to that persuasion.
>
> (See QUOTATIONS, p. 44)

Princes should strive to imitate the examples set by great rulers of the past, even if that means setting lofty goals. This way, if a prince fails to meet those lofty goals, his actions will nevertheless enhance his reputation as a great or powerful ruler.

One way that rulers acquire states is through their own prowess, meaning their own abilities, rather than the good fortune of noble birth, inheritance, or lucky circumstances. Relying on one's personal prowess is a very difficult method of acquiring a state. However, a state acquired by a ruler's natural skill will prove easier to maintain control over. Examples of rulers who triumphed on the strength of their own powers include Moses, Cyrus, Romulus, and Theseus.

Rulers who rely on prowess instead of fortune are generally more successful in holding power over states because they can meet the challenge of establishing a new order. Nothing is more dangerous or difficult than introducing a new order. This is because those who benefited from the old order will fiercely oppose the prince who tries to introduce a new order, whereas those who stand to benefit from the imposition of a new order will offer only lukewarm support. A prince who relies on his ability to persuade others to support him will be unable to succeed against such opposition. However, a prince who relies on his own prowess and can "force the issue" will usually succeed. At times, "forc[ing] the issue" might literally mean the use of force. This can be dangerous, but if the ruler succeeds in his use of force, he will become strong, secure, and respected.

ᴊMMARY — CHAPTER VII: CONCERNING NEW PRINCIPALITIES ACQUIRED WITH THE ARMS AND FORTUNES OF OTHERS

Sometimes private citizens become princes purely by good fortune. Such people buy their way into power, receive favors from someone else in power, or bribe soldiers. Such princes are weak not only because fortune can be capricious and unstable, but also because they do not know how to maintain their position. They do not have loyal troops who are devoted to them. They do not know how to deal with problems, command troops, or keep their power in the face of opposition. Princes who succeed on their own prowess have built a strong foundation for themselves. Princes who succeed due to the sway of fortune or the goodwill of others lack such a foundation from which to rule and will have difficulty building a foundation quickly enough to prevent power from slipping out of their hands. Thus, although princes who rely on fortune reach their position easily, maintaining that position is extremely difficult.

Laying a solid foundation is a crucial prerequisite for maintaining power. A prince must eliminate rival leaders and win the favor of their followers. Machiavelli cites the life of Cesare Borgia (also called Duke Valentino) as an example. The son of Pope Alexander VI, Borgia was a man of great courage and high intentions. He was made duke of Romagna through the good fortune that his father, as Pope Alexander VI, had amassed a great deal of power. However, he was unable to maintain his rule, even though he made competent attempts to consolidate his new power. His efforts included the use of force in the strategic conquest of foreign lands. He tried to make himself loved and feared by his subjects. He wiped out disloyal troops and established a loyal army, and he maintained a friendly yet cautious relationship with other kings and princes. Despite all his efforts, he was unable to complete the consolidation of his power when his father died, and his good fortune was reversed. He did, however, lay a strong foundation for future rule, as only a man of great prowess could.

ANALYSIS — CHAPTERS V–VII

The coldhearted, calculating logic for which Machiavelli is renowned shines through in Chapter V. His argument that devastating a region is often the most reliable way of securing power does not even attempt to address the moral or ethical objections to his advice. His rationale is strictly pragmatic: the only reason to spare the institutions of newly conquered states is that keeping old institutions alive might help keep citizens happy, subdued, and submissive under the new ruler.

Moreover, in Chapter V, Machiavelli sets out his conception of the natural state of a populace. He writes that most subjects are "used to obeying" and that they cannot live as free subjects without someone telling them what to do. This argument echoes Machiavelli's assertion in Chapter III that men are naturally disposed to "old ways of life" and therefore harbor an inclination to follow tradition. These passages underline the assumption that men are, by nature, followers. Even rulers are followers to some extent: Machiavelli notes at the start of Chapter VI that aspiring princes are always inclined to "imitate" the examples of great men.

Machiavelli imagines subjects who are self-interested, but not to an extreme degree. They are not concerned with forms of enlightenment or self-improvement, yet they still notice (and appreciate) improvements in their overall well-being. Though generally obedient and complacent, they will not hesitate to rise up against their ruler should he offend them. *The Prince* devotes little space to the concerns of subjects, and Machiavelli's picture of the common people, though detailed, is not complex. Louis XIV's famous statement, "L'Etat, c'est moi" ("The state is me"), accords with the philosophy espoused in *The Prince*: The ruler is the state, and the state is ruler. The people hardly matter.

This idea does not necessarily contradict Machiavelli's view that the effectiveness of government depends on the firm support of its people. Rather, it implies that Machiavelli is not concerned with understanding what motivates the people to lend support to a ruler. The only important question is whether such support exists.

The primary virtue of Machiavelli's prince is self-reliance. A prince who manages to gain power by relying on his own prowess will succeed at maintaining power because his prowess will have built him a firm foundation for ruling. He will have the loyalty of his army and the respect of those he has conquered and the leaders of surrounding principalities. He therefore will be better equipped to deal with problems and difficulties, without relying on the help of others. Thus, the more self-reliant the prince, the more he will prove capable of success.

CHAPTERS VIII–IX

SUMMARY — CHAPTER VIII: CONCERNING THOSE WHO BECOME PRINCES BY EVIL MEANS

Machiavelli continues to describe the ways that a man can become a prince. In addition to fortune and prowess, criminal acts or the approval of his fellow citizens can facilitate a man's rise to power.

Those who come to power by crime kill fellow citizens and betray friends. They are "treacherous, pitiless, and irreligious." Princes who commit criminal acts can achieve power, but never glory.

King Agathocles of Syracuse is an example of a man who rose to power through crime. Agathocles was a common citizen who joined the militia, rose to a leading rank in the army, and then assembled a meeting of the senate at which he ordered his men to kill all the senators and to install him in power. Agathocles' reign was characterized by constant difficulties and threats to his power. However, he withstood them and maintained his rule. Once in power, Agathocles proved as competent as any eminent commander, but the severity of the crimes he committed during his ascension preclude his being considered great. Cruelty, which is itself evil, can be used well if it is applied once at the outset, and thereafter only employed in self-defense and for the greater good of one's subjects. Regular and frequent perpetration of cruel actions earns a ruler infamy. If a prince comes to power by crime and wishes to be successful, he, like Agathocles, must only use cruelty in the first sense.

Therefore, when a prince decides to seize a state, he must determine how much injury to inflict. He needs to strike all at once and then refrain from further atrocities. In this way, his subjects will eventually forget the violence and cruelty. Gradually, resentment will fade, and the people will come to appreciate the resulting benefits of the prince's rule. Most important, a prince should be consistent in the way he treats his subjects.

SUMMARY — CHAPTER IX: CONCERNING THE CIVIL PRINCIPALITY

The other way a prince can come to power is through the favor of his fellow citizens. Princes who rise through this route are heads of what Machiavelli calls constitutional principalities.

Machiavelli argues that every city is populated by two groups of citizens: common people and nobles. The common people are naturally disposed to avoid domination and oppression by the nobles.

The nobles are naturally disposed to dominate and oppress the common people. The opposition between the two groups results in the establishment of either a principality, a free city, or anarchy.

The power to form a principality lies with either the nobles or the people. If the nobles realize they cannot dominate the people, they will try to strengthen their position by making one of the nobles a prince. They hope to accomplish their own ends through the prince's authority. The people will follow the same course of action; if they realize they cannot withstand the nobles, they will make one of the people a prince and hope to be protected by the prince's authority.

A prince placed in power by nobles will find it more difficult to maintain his position because those who surround him will consider themselves his equals and his selection as prince arbitrary. However, a prince created by the people stands alone at the top. Not only are nobles much harder to satisfy than the people, they are less honest in their motives because they seek to oppress the people. The people, on the other hand, only seek to be left alone. If the people are hostile to the prince, the worst that can happen is desertion. However, if the nobles are hostile, the prince can expect both desertion and active opposition. Nobles are astute and cunning and always safeguard their interests.

Nobles will either become dependent on the prince or remain independent of his control. A prince should honor and love those nobles who have become dependent on him. Nobles who remain independent are either timid or ambitious. Timid nobles are benign, but a prince should be wary of ambitious nobles, since they will become enemies in times of adversity.

A prince created by the people must retain the people's friendship, a fairly easy task. A prince created by the nobles must still try to win over the people's affection, because they can serve as protection from hostile nobles. Benevolence is the best way to maintain the mandate of the people. If people expect hostility from a prince but instead receive kindness and favors, they feel a great obligation to their prince.

Principalities usually face difficulties when switching from a government with limited powers to one that is more absolute. To make this transition, a prince can either rule directly or through magistrates. The prince is more vulnerable in the latter case because he is dependent on the will of his magistrates. In times of adversity, the magistrates may depose him, through direct action against him or simply by disobeying his orders. Moreover, if the magistrates do revolt, the prince will be unable to assume absolute power, because the people are accustomed to obeying the magistrates rather than the prince. In prosperous times, it is fashionable to declare allegiance to a prince. But during times of danger, trusted men become scarce. A wise prince must find a way to ensure that his citizens are always dependent on his authority. Thus, they will always remain loyal.

ANALYSIS — CHAPTERS VIII–IX

These chapters describe how different types of princes should establish power, within a state's environment of fluctuating power dynamics. Machiavelli makes an eloquent argument for the importance of a domestic power base. He does not hesitate to acknowledge the necessity of cruelty and crime in establishing this power and even explains how to use cruelty most effectively. He does not advise moderation in the degree of cruelty used, but rather a limit on how long extreme cruelty is to be employed. That is, Machiavelli does not say that princes must be cruel but not extremely cruel. Instead, he argues that cruel acts must be committed as necessary, but all at once and then ceased, so that the populace will forget them. This kind of argument is extremely pragmatic and ignores all questions of right and wrong. Taking historical examples as the basis for his argument, Machiavelli simply describes how power has effectively been deployed and consolidated in the past, and does not assume that human nature will take a turn for the better in the future.

Even when princes do not need to rely on cruelty, Machiavelli still describes a necessary, dangerous game of internal politics, which involves the pitting of one group of citizens against another. As a guiding principle, a prince's power invariably depends on internal support. Whether a prince uses cruelty or benevolence to obtain that support is secondary to the necessity of gaining the support itself.

Machiavelli is more than the amoral pragmatist he is sometimes made out to be. The distinction made between power and glory indicates that, in Machiavelli's view, some princes are better than others. While any prince can achieve and maintain power, glory remains a more elusive goal. Although Machiavelli is primarily concerned with how princes perform as rulers, he also gives an assessment of the different kinds of princes. Machiavelli's view is that the prince who rises and survives by means of treachery and the prince who succeeds by his innate prowess are both technically princes. But he also admits that the two are not equal in honor or glory, and, perhaps, even moral worth.

Moreover, Machiavelli also characterizes the use of cruelty as "evil." In some cases, cruelty is a necessary evil, and using it can be justified in the interests of some greater public good, like internal stability or protection from invasion. Yet Machiavelli's very recognition of the intrinsic immorality of cruel behavior contradicts the depiction of *The Prince* as a completely amoral book.

Machiavelli's description of class conflict in Chapter IX, which states that there is an inevitable tension between common people and nobles, is also worth noting. Superficially, this statement brings Machiavelli in line with political philosophers such as Karl Marx, who view class conflict as an inevitable aspect of civilized society. But Machiavelli's description of "classes" is much less sophisticated than that of Marx. More fundamentally, Machiavelli does not see class conflict as a driving force behind political structures. Rather, it is one of a number of challenges that a prince must learn to negotiate if he is to be successful. Consequently, in describing the great struggle between commoners and nobles, Machiavelli does not side with either group. Instead, his stance is more detached, focusing only on a hypothetical prince's relationship with these groups.

One of the most significant components of Machiavelli's argumentative style is his use of definition by division, a rhetorical device that can be quite convincing. This device can be described schematically as "A prince must accomplish X. Accomplishing X entails either method Y or method Z. Y is preferable to Z, so a prince should choose method Y." It is a logical and practical line of reasoning, but if the original assumption linking the chain of logic is fallacious, then all the conclusions that follow are necessarily questionable. If Y and Z aren't the only way to accomplish X, then the course of action that Machiavelli proposes for a prince is not necessarily the best possible option. One might ask, for example, whether there are other ways of becoming a prince besides prowess, fortune, crime, and favor. And it may be possible that there are other, more various factions within cities besides commoners and nobles. For that matter, it can be argued that there are other more subtle ways to win support than cruelty and benevolence.

Chapters X–XI

Summary — Chapter X: How the Strength of All Principalities Should Be Measured

Although a prince should always aim to keep an army of size and strength equaling that of any aggressor, it is just as important to maintain defenses and fortifications. These defensive preparations not only provide security but also deter enemies from attacking.

Some might argue that if an enemy lays siege to a fortified city, the people inside, upon witnessing their countryside pillaged and possessions destroyed, will turn against their prince. But a prince who has made adequate defensive preparations can actually inspire his subjects during such times. To do so, he must convince the people that the hardships are only temporary and, more importantly, create feelings of patriotism and enthusiasm for the city's defense. This way, when the siege is over, the grateful and obliged people will love the prince all the more.

Summary — Chapter XI: Concerning Ecclesiastical Principalities

Ecclesiastical principalities, regions under the control of the Catholic Church, are different from other kinds of principalities. Taking control of these principalities is difficult, requiring either unusual good fortune or prowess. Machiavelli sarcastically remarks that principles of religion, rather than governments, rule ecclesiastical principalities, so the prince does not even need to govern. Ecclesiastical principalities do not need to be defended, and their subjects require no administration. Nonetheless, these states are always secure and happy. Since these principalities are "sustained by higher powers which the human mind cannot comprehend," delving further into why this is the case would be presumptuous.

It is useful, however, to look at how the Church has obtained its great temporal power. Italy was once divided among the pope and the city-states of Venice, Naples, Milan, and Florence. Each of these powers was wary of the others and prevented the intervention of any foreign power. Papal power was fairly weak during this time, due to disagreement among the Roman barons and the short duration of papacies. But Popes Alexander VI and Julius II greatly increased the power of the Church by using armed force to weaken the other factions, accumulating wealth to strengthen the Church's own position, and nurturing factionalism within any remaining factions.

Thus, the current Church, under the leadership of Pope Leo X, has been made strong through the force of arms. It is now hoped that Pope Leo will use his goodness and virtue to maintain its power.

ANALYSIS — CHAPTERS X–XI

Although Chapter X focuses partly on maintaining the well-being of the people in a city during a period of difficulty, Machiavelli views this only as a necessary step in making the city itself strong and immune from attack. One surprising characteristic of *The Prince* is how completely it defines the city as an entity existing to serve its ruler rather than its populace. The discussion of fortification emphasizes this conception of the city: obtaining the support of the people is not a goal in itself but rather a means for ensuring that the city remain fortified and resistant to foreign conquest. The purpose of convincing the people that their hardships are temporary, for example, is not to lighten the burden of the people whose city is besieged, but rather a way to ensure the defense of the city. The ultimate goal is not happiness but patriotism: the defense of the state and its ruler. While Machiavelli often advocates the use of military force, he also recognizes that military strength alone cannot maintain a state's strength. Although the fortification of cities has a military value, Machiavelli focuses on fortification as a tool by which a prince can solidify popular support in times of war or siege.

Chapter XI may initially seem inconsistent with the rest of Machiavelli's writing. His acknowledgment that ecclesiastical principalities are not subject to the historical patterns he observes, and his description of their immunity from bad rulers and war, initially seem to point to a respect for religion and acknowledgment of a higher moral plane on which a state can exist. But Machiavelli's remarks in this chapter are bitterly ironic—he actually opposes the presence of the Church in politics altogether, a view that he makes explicit in his *Discourses*. In reality, Machiavelli understands ecclesiastical principalities to be examples of the effective consolidation of power, much in the same way as the examples of successful princes that he cites. He focuses on the factors that ultimately led to the Catholic Church gaining control over Italian principalities, and reveals that these factors were not essentially different than those used by other princes to gain power. Like other princes, the Church used armed force, the accumulation of wealth, and astute political strategy in order to gain control. Even though Machiavelli opens the chapter professing that ecclesiastical principalities exist in their own category, ultimately he views them just as he does any other state.

Chapters XII–XIV

Summary — Chapter XII: Concerning Various Kinds of Troops, and Especially Mercenaries

All princes must build on strong foundations. The two essential components of a strong state are good laws and good armies. Good laws cannot exist without good armies. The presence of a good army, however, indicates the presence of good laws.

There are three types of armies: a prince's own troops, mercenary troops, and auxiliary troops. Mercenary and auxiliary troops are useless and dangerous. Mercenaries are "disunited, undisciplined, ambitious, and faithless." Because their only motivation is monetary, they are generally not effective in battle and have low morale. Mercenary commanders are either skilled or unskilled. Unskilled commanders are worthless, but skilled commanders cannot be trusted to suppress their own ambition. It is far more preferable for a prince to command his own army.

Historically, dependence on mercenaries ruined Italy. During the breakup of Italy, which the Church supported in hopes of increasing its own stature, many townships hired mercenaries because they had little experience in military matters. Since the mercenaries were more concerned with increasing their own prestige and status than with taking risks or accomplishing military objectives, the conflicts between these mercenary forces devolved into a series of ineffective, staged, pseudo-battles, ultimately degrading Italy's political and military might.

Summary — Chapter XIII: Concerning Auxiliary, Mixed, and Native Forces

Auxiliary troops—armies borrowed from a more powerful state—are as useless as mercenaries. Although they often fight well, a prince who calls on auxiliaries places himself in a no-win situation. If the auxiliaries fail, he is defenseless, whereas if the auxiliaries are successful, he still owes his victory to the power of another. Auxiliary troops are often skilled and organized, yet their first loyalty is to another ruler. Thus, they pose an even more dangerous threat to the prince than mercenaries.

If a prince does not command his own native troops, the principality can never be secure. Depending on outside armies is essentially the same as depending on good fortune. The use of auxiliaries and mercenaries is effective during prosperous times, but in times of adversity, reliance on borrowed troops, like reliance on fortune, is a perilous liability.

SUMMARY — CHAPTER XIV: A PRINCE'S CONCERN IN MILITARY MATTERS

> *A prince must have no other objective, no other*
> *thought, nor take up any profession but that of war.*
> *(See* QUOTATIONS, *p. 45)*

The only thing a prince needs to study is the art of war. This is the primary discipline of the ruler. Mastery of this discipline can make even a common citizen a great ruler. The easiest way to lose a state is by neglecting the art of war. The best way to win a state is to be skilled in the art of war.

Machiavelli offers an analogy, asking us to picture two men: one armed, the other unarmed. It would not be reasonable to expect the armed man to obey the unarmed man. Nor would it be reasonable to expect the unarmed man to feel safe and secure if his servants are armed. The unarmed man will be suspicious of the armed man, and the armed man will feel contempt for the unarmed man, so cooperation will be impossible. A prince who does not understand warfare attempting to lead an army is like the unarmed man trying to lead the armed.

The prince must spend all of his time studying the art of war. This study is both a physical and mental process. The prince must train his body to hardships and learn to hunt wildlife. He must study geography and its effect on battle strategy. He must read history and study the actions of great leaders. A prince must prepare rigorously during peacetime in order to be well prepared for wartime.

ANALYSIS — CHAPTERS XII–XIV

Machiavelli's famous statement that "the presence of sound military forces indicates the presence of sound laws" is a succinct description of the relationship between war and the formation of states in *The Prince*. Warcraft is conventionally understood as the component of statesmanship that involves the expansion of the state by conquering neighbors and establishing colonies. But Machiavelli argues that successful warcraft is not just one component among other equally important components of statesmanship. Instead, it is the very foundation upon which all states are built. Machiavelli defines the term "warcraft" quite broadly. For him, the idea encompasses more than just the direct use of military force. It comprises international diplomacy, domestic politics, tactical strategy, geographic mastery, and historical analysis. Perhaps influenced by the context in which he was writing, Machiavelli viewed war as something that never could disappear completely, nor did he even conceive of the absence of war as a goal. Even in the most peaceful of times, the clouds of war always threaten.

Machiavelli's advocacy of the use of internal troops, rather than mercenaries or auxiliaries, follows naturally from previous chapters, in which he asserts the need for self-reliance and the projection of power. Historical anecdotes are prevalent throughout these chapters. Machiavelli's reference to Italy in the context of mercenaries is significant, since he wrote *The Prince* partly to help Italy become more stable and powerful in the face of its aggressive neighbors. However, in these chapters Machiavelli does not refer to Italy's history more than that of other countries, so it is not readily apparent at this point in the book that he intends to single out his home country.

In Chapter XIV, Machiavelli shifts his focus from the role of the prince to the personality of the prince. While previous chapters have focused upon the correct actions for the prince to perform and the characteristics of a strong state, in this chapter Machiavelli examines the psychology of a good prince. Machiavelli writes that "the prince ought to read history, and reflect upon the deeds of outstanding men, . . . examine the causes of their victories and defeats, and thereby learn to emulate the former and avoid the latter." The portrait of an ideal prince does not describe a ruler who equally values politics, philosophy, and art as aspects of his rule, but one who focuses exclusively on the military strength of the state that he governs.

Chapters XV–XVII

Summary — Chapter XV: Concerning Things for Which Men, and Princes Especially, Are Praised or Censured

Machiavelli turns the discussion from the strength of states and principalities to the correct behavior of the prince. Machiavelli admits that this subject has been treated by others, but he argues that an original set of practical—rather than theoretical—rules is needed. Other philosophers have conceived republics built upon an idealized notion of how men should live rather than how men actually live. But truth strays far from the expectations of imagined ideals. Specifically, men never live every part of their life virtuously. A prince should not concern himself with living virtuously, but rather with acting so as to achieve the most practical benefit.

In general, some personal characteristics will earn men praise, others condemnation. Courage, compassion, faith, craftiness, and generosity number among the qualities that receive praise. Cowardice, cruelty, stubbornness, and miserliness are usually met with condemnation. Ideally, a prince would possess all the qualities deemed "good" by other men. But this expectation is unrealistic. A prince's first job is to safeguard the state, and harboring "bad" characteristics is sometimes necessary for this end. Such vices are truly evil if they endanger the state, but when vices are employed in the proper interests of the state, a prince must not be influenced by condemnation from other men.

SUMMARY — CHAPTER XVI: LIBERALITY AND PARSIMONY

> *Of all the things he must guard against, hatred and contempt come first, and liberality leads to both.*
> (See QUOTATIONS, *p. 45*)

Liberality, or generosity, is a quality that many men admire. But if a prince develops a reputation for generosity, he will ruin his state. A reputation for generosity requires outward lavishness, which eventually depletes all of the prince's resources. In the end, the prince will be forced to burden his people with excessive taxes in order to raise the money to maintain his reputation for generosity. Ultimately, the prince's liberality will make the people despise and resent him. Moreover, any prince who attempts to change his reputation for generosity will immediately develop a reputation for being a miser.

A parsimonious, or ungenerous, prince may be perceived as miserly in the beginning, but he will eventually earn a reputation for generosity. A prince who is thrifty and frugal will eventually have enough funds to defend against aggression and fund projects without having to tax the people unduly.

In history, the actions of Pope Julius II, the present king of France, and the present king of Spain all support the view that parsimony enables the prince to accomplish great things. Some might argue that successful leaders have come to power and sustained their rule by virtue of their generosity, such as Caesar. But if Caesar had not been killed, he would have found that maintaining his rule required moderating his spending.

In sum, generosity is self-defeating. Generosity uses up resources and prevents further generosity. While parsimony might lead to ignominy, generosity will eventually lead to hatred.

SUMMARY — CHAPTER XVII: CONCERNING CRUELTY: WHETHER IT IS BETTER TO BE LOVED THAN TO BE FEARED, OR THE REVERSE

Compassion, like generosity, is usually admired. But a prince must be careful that he does not show compassion unwisely. If a prince is too compassionate, and does not adequately punish disloyal subjects, he creates an atmosphere of disorder, since his subjects take the liberty to do what they please—even to the extremes of murder and theft. Crime harms the entire community, whereas executions harm only the individuals who commit crimes. Some measure of cruelty is necessary to maintain order. But a prince should be careful in his exercise of cruelty, tempering it with humanity and prudence.

Machiavelli then asks whether being feared or loved is preferable. Ideally, a prince should be both loved and feared, but this state of affairs is difficult to attain. Forced to make a choice, it is much better to be feared than loved. This is because men, by nature, are "ungrateful, fickle, dissembling, anxious to flee danger, and covetous of gain." In times of remote danger, they are willing to take risks for their prince, but if the danger is real, they turn against their prince. It is easy to break a bond of love when the situation arises, but the fear of punishment is always effective, regardless of the situation.

When inducing fear, however, a prince must be careful to avoid inducing hatred. He must make sure that any executions are properly justified. Above all, a prince should never confiscate the property of his subjects or take their women, since these actions are most likely to breed hatred. If a prince must confiscate property, he must make sure he has a convincing reason. With one's army, however, there is no such thing as too much cruelty. Keeping an army disciplined and united requires cruelty, even inhuman cruelty.

ANALYSIS — CHAPTERS XV–XVII

Chapter XV attacks the conceptions of virtue proposed by classical philosophers. Machiavelli criticizes the concept of a "good life," the

Aristotelian doctrine that demands virtuous actions in all types of behavior. Machiavelli debunks Aristotle's metaphysical approach to politics by arguing that metaphysics is inconsistent with the real world. Ultimately, a philosophy must be judged by its practical consequences. Because virtue, as an abstract concept, does not concern itself with such consequences, it can never serve as an effective guide for political action. Machiavelli's definition of virtue is not the same as that of classical philosophers. While Aristotle and others define virtue in relation to a highest good, Machiavelli defines it simply as that which receives the praise of others. Thus, generosity is a virtue only because other people praise it.

From this premise, Machiavelli builds a case for the necessity of committing certain crimes. A prince, if he truly wishes to safeguard his state, will inevitably be forced to act in a manner that others consider evil or deplorable. Although Machiavelli only mentions cruelty and stinginess in Chapters XVI and XVII, the argument could extend to other so-called vices, such as stubbornness or cowardice. The mind of Machiavelli's prince is cold and calculating, concerned with ends rather than means. Virtually any action that contributes to the overall goal of maintaining control of the state is acceptable to him.

Unlike the previous chapters, which contain specific instructions regarding domestic, international, and military affairs, these chapters deal with general trends of popular opinion that might affect the prince's actions. Machiavelli urges the prince not to worry too much about what others might think of his actions and to act only in the way that will result in the best practical advantage—which will often garner greater approval from other people in the long run. In most cases, the prince must favor miserliness over generosity, and cruelty over benevolence. But Machiavelli does not advocate wholesale cruelty or a complete lack of generosity; it is possible for a prince to be too miserly or too cruel. A prince might choose cowardice over courage—for example, fleeing a palace under siege instead of remaining and rallying the people—but the effectiveness of either option depends on the surrounding circumstances. The advice put forth in these chapters is substantially less concrete than that offered in previous chapters.

Machiavelli's oft-quoted line "Anyone compelled to choose will find far greater security in being feared than in being loved" is sometimes misinterpreted to suggest that a prince need not worry about public opinion. But Machiavelli explicitly argues the contrary: it is critical that a prince avoid the hatred of his subjects. The statement is less radical than it might seem. People, states Machiavelli, are all self-interested to a certain degree. During difficult times, this sense of self-interest is stronger than any sense of obligation toward the ruler or the state. No matter how strongly they might love their prince, people will not follow orders if it means sacrificing their own well-being. The only motivating factor that can guarantee citizens' obedience to a prince's orders is the threat of punishment.

Although Machiavelli's conclusions may seem disturbing, if we consider contemporary society, we might conclude that little has changed since the era of *The Prince*. Even today, while some people certainly follow laws because they feel that they have a moral obligation to do so, or because they respect the institution that makes the laws, many others follow them simply because they fear the punishment that comes with breaking those laws. Supporters of the death penalty in the United States usually argue that the use of capital punishment acts as a deterrent, discouraging the general populace from committing capital crimes.

CHAPTERS XVIII–XIX

SUMMARY — CHAPTER XVIII: IN WHAT WAY PRINCES SHOULD KEEP THEIR WORD

Machiavelli acknowledges that a prince who honors his word is generally praised by others. But historical experience demonstrates that princes achieve the most success when they are crafty, cunning, and able to trick others. There are two ways of fighting: by law or by force. Laws come naturally to men, force comes naturally to beasts. In order to succeed, the prince must learn how to fight both with laws and with force—he must become half man and half beast.

When a prince uses force, he acts like a beast. He must learn to act like two types of beasts: lions and foxes. A fox is defenseless against wolves; a lion is defenseless against traps. A prince must learn to act like both the fox and the lion: he must learn, like the fox, how to frighten off wolves and, like the lion, how to recognize the traps. In dealing with people, a prince must break his promises when they put him at a disadvantage and when the reasons for which he made the promises no longer exist. In any case, promises are never something on which a prince can rely, since men are by nature wretched and deceitful. A prince should be a master of deception.

However, a prince must be careful to exude a virtuous aura that belies his deceitful mind. Pope Alexander VI was one ruler who excelled at this art. A prince should present the appearance of being a compassionate, trustworthy, kind, guileless, and pious ruler. Of course, actually possessing all these virtues is neither possible nor desirable. But so long as a prince appears to act virtuously, most men will believe in his virtue. If the populace believes the prince to be virtuous, it will be easier for him to maintain his state. Moreover, men will judge their prince solely on appearance and results. Thus, it doesn't matter to the people that a prince may occasionally employ evil to achieve his goal. So long as a prince appears virtuous and is successful in running the state, he will be regarded as virtuous.

Summary — Chapter XIX: The Need to Avoid Contempt and Hatred

A prince must avoid being hated and despised at all costs. A prince may be criticized for a lack of virtue, but he will never be hated for it. However, a prince will be hated if he takes the property or women of his subjects. A prince must also avoid robbing his subjects of their honor. A prince will be despised if he has a reputation for being fickle, frivolous, effeminate, cowardly, or irresolute. If a prince is regarded highly by his subjects, he will be shielded from conspiracies and open attacks.

A prince should worry about two things: internal insurrection from his subjects and external threats from foreign powers. Defending against foreign enemies requires a strong army and good allies. A strong army always leads to good allies.

A prince can defend against internal insurrection by making sure he is not hated or scorned by the people. This is a powerful defense against conspiracies. A conspirator will have the courage to proceed with his conspiracy only if he believes the people will be satisfied when he kills the ruler. But if the people would be outraged by the ruler's death, the conspirators will never have the gall to carry out the conspiracy. By default, conspiracies are at a disadvantage. They require the support of many people, each of whom faces severe punishment if the conspiracy is discovered. Furthermore, each of these people can profit richly by informing the prince about the conspiracy. A prince has on his side the entire government, his allies and the laws of the state. If he secures the goodwill of the people, he seems invulnerable in the eyes of conspirators.

Whenever possible, a prince should delegate the administration of unpopular laws to others and keep in his own power the distribution of favors.

Sometimes it will not be possible to avoid being hated by some members of the populace. If it is not possible for the prince to avoid being hated, he must make it his first priority to escape the hatred of the most powerful parties. In many instances, this will mean ensuring good standing within the ranks of the military. But a prince should not worry too much about satisfying the demands of the troops, especially if it comes at the expense of the people. A number of later Roman emperors were overthrown due to excessive cruelty performed for the sake of their army. The exception was Septimius Severus, who, emulating both lion and fox, overawed both his army and his people. Most present-day princes need not fear their armies and should be attentive to the people.

ANALYSIS — CHAPTERS XVIII–XIX

The argument in Chapter XVIII that princes should be prepared to break promises for practical advantage develops Machiavelli's position on virtue and vice. Machiavelli does not argue that a prince should actively avoid doing what is good but that, if necessary, a prince must be prepared to act unethically. He does not advise ruthlessness for its own sake, but rather indicates the perhaps unfortunate necessity of ruthlessness in leadership.

Although the proposal that a prince must exude a false aura of virtue may seem merely one more kind of deception that the prince must learn to master, Machiavelli's advice here remains valid even in contemporary politics. Although some of Machiavelli's writing might be dismissed as irrelevant to democratic political life, his perceptive analysis of the importance of image is still accurate. Machiavelli points out that image is as important as action, and that rulers must manipulate the perceptions of the populace to appear as other than who they really are. A prince should eagerly take credit for successes and place responsibility for unpopular laws on the shoulders of nobles or lesser officials. Of course, the prince's aim is not to be loved, but merely to avoid being hated. Although Machiavelli's prince rules in an autocratic state, he must nonetheless practice the kind of politics of image demanded within republics and democracies.

These chapters give us further insight into Machiavelli's view of human nature. Men are naturally deceitful and untrustworthy.

THE PRINCE ❦ 37

They are likely to break promises. They are easily impressed by appearances and results. They are selfish but somewhat naïve. They respect and praise virtue, but most do not possess it themselves. These assumptions about the basic behaviors and attitudes of the general population underlie all of Machiavelli's suggestions for the actions of princes. If the populace is intelligent, well-educated, and acutely aware of history, the prince will not be able to generate the deceptive image that Machiavelli argues is integral to successful leadership. Although these assumptions may or may not be true, Machiavelli is much more willing to make unsupported generalizations about human nature than about history. His historical examples are painstakingly accurate and demonstrate Machiavelli's great erudition. But he does not support his descriptions of human behavior with the same wealth of evidence.

Machiavelli consistently refers to the ruler as "he" and assumes that his gender is male. One could dismiss this fact as simply a consequence of history—rulers during Machiavelli's time were almost always men. But Machiavelli's association of leadership with masculinity extends beyond simple historical context. He also writes that a prince should avoid behaving effeminately at all costs, and associates effeminacy with cowardice and fickleness. The implication is that manliness is a prerequisite for ruling. Machiavelli notes that Alexander was thought to be ruled by his mother, and therefore deemed effeminate, a perception that led to his downfall. Machiavelli's definition of manliness encompasses the "harder" virtues, such as courage and decisiveness, in contrast with "softer" virtues like compassion and generosity. In this sense, although cruelty is not a virtue, the ability to act cruelly whenever necessary can be considered manly, and, therefore, virtuous.

CHAPTERS XX–XXIII

SUMMARY — CHAPTER XX: WHETHER FORTRESSES AND MANY OTHER EXPEDIENTS THAT PRINCES COMMONLY EMPLOY ARE USEFUL OR NOT

To defend against internal insurrection, princes have used a variety of strategies. Some have divided towns, some have disarmed the populace, some have tried to woo disloyal subjects, and others have built or destroyed fortresses. The effectiveness of each of these policies depends on the individual conditions, but a few generalizations can be made.

Historically, new princes have never prevented their subjects from having weapons. Arming subjects fosters loyalty among the people and defends the prince. Disarming subjects will breed distrust, which leads to civil animosity. But if a prince annexes a state, he must disarm his new subjects. He can allow his supporters in the new state to keep their arms, but eventually they must also be made weaker. The best arrangement is to have the prince's own soldiers occupying the new state. However, weakening an annexed territory by encouraging factionalism only makes it more easily captured by foreigners, as the Venetians learned.

Princes become great by defeating opposition. Thus, one way they can enhance their stature is to cunningly foster opposition that can be easily overcome. Moreover, fostering subversion in a new state will help reveal the motives of potential conspirators.

Some princes have chosen to build fortresses to curb rebellion. Others have destroyed them, in order to maintain control in newly acquired states. The usefulness of fortresses depends on the specific circumstances. But a fortress will not be able to protect a prince if he is hated by his subjects. The issue is not whether a prince should build a fortress. Rather, a prince should not put all his trust in a fortress, neglecting the attitudes of his people.

SUMMARY — CHAPTER XXI: WHAT A PRINCE MUST DO TO BE ESTEEMED

Great enterprises and noble examples are two ways for a prince to earn prestige. Examples of great campaigns include those of King Ferdinand of Spain, who skillfully used his military to attack Granada, Africa, Italy, and France. These campaigns focused his people's attention and prevented attacks against Ferdinand.

Nobility can be achieved by the grand public display of rewards and punishments. Above all, princes should win a reputation for being men of outstanding ability.

A prince can also win prestige by declaring himself an ally of one side of a conflict. Neutrality alienates both the victor and the loser. The victor sees the neutral prince as a doubtful friend; the loser sees the neutral prince as weak coward. Someone who is not your friend will always request that you remain neutral, while a true friend will always ask you for your armed support. A prince can escape short-term danger through neutrality, but at the cost of long-term grief. Instead, a prince should boldly declare support for one side.

If the prince allies with someone stronger than himself, and this ally wins, then the prince protects himself through the alliance, because the victor will feel an obligation to the prince. If this stronger ally loses, at least the prince will win the protection and shelter of the ally. If the prince is stronger than either opponent, an alliance essentially means the destruction of one side through the help of another.

If possible, a prince should avoid siding with an ally whose power is greater than his own. Victory in this situation will only put the prince at mercy of that ally. However, sometimes such an alliance is unavoidable. Because of these instances, a prince should never believe that a completely safe course exists. Instead, he should assess the risks presented by all options and choose the least risky course of action. A prudent prince can assess threats and accept the lesser evil.

A prince should encourage his citizens to excel in their occupations, and live their lives in peace. Thus, a prince should never discourage or excessively tax private acquisition or prosperous commerce. Instead, a prince should reward those who contribute to the overall prosperity of the state. Such rewards might include annual city-wide festivals and personal visits with guilds and family groups.

SUMMARY — CHAPTER XXII: CONCERNING THE PRINCE'S MINISTERS

The selection of ministers is a critical task because ministers give visitors their first impression of the prince. Wise and loyal ministers contribute to the image of a wise prince. Inversely, incompetent and disloyal ministers give the prince the image of incompetence.

There are three types of intellect that men can possess: the ability to understand things independently, the ability to appreciate another person's ability to understand things, and the ability to do neither. The first kind is best, the second acceptable, and the third useless. If a prince possesses at least the second kind of intellect, he can judge whether his ministers' actions are good or bad.

If a minister thinks more of himself than of the prince and does everything for personal profit, then he is a bad minister. A prince should recognize this state of affairs. Good ministers, however, should be rewarded to maintain their loyalty. Rewards can be paid in money, honor, and expanded responsibilities. It is crucial for a prince to have a confident relationship with his ministers.

SUMMARY — CHAPTER XXIII: HOW TO AVOID FLATTERERS

Flatterers present a danger to any ruler because it is natural for powerful men to become self-absorbed. The best way to defend against such people is to convince them that you are not offended by the truth. But if everyone can speak to the prince, the prince will lose respect. A prince should allow only wise advisers to speak with him, and only when he specifically requests their advice. A prince should not listen to anyone else and should be firm in his decisions. Vacillation will lead to a loss of respect.

A prince must always seek advice. But he must seek it only when he wants it, not when others thrust it upon him. Most important, a prince must always be skeptical about the advice he receives, constantly questioning and probing. If he ever discovers that someone is concealing the truth from him, he must punish that person severely. In the end, no matter how intelligent a prince's advisers might be, a prince is doomed if he lacks intelligence of his own. Wise princes should be honored for good actions proceeding from good advice.

ANALYSIS — CHAPTERS XX–XXIII

Chapter XX returns to the issue of popular insurrection and how a prince should defend against it. Machiavelli argues that a prince must avoid hatred and suppress opposition before it can gain sufficient momentum to disrupt his rule. Also, he does not base his assessment of fortresses on their military value. Fortresses can be worthwhile or worthless depending on the individual circumstances. The attitude of the people outweighs the value of any physical structure. Machiavelli places emphasis on a distinctly nonmilitary aspect in his discussion of fortresses, a building traditionally associated with the military, indicating his broad interpretation of warcraft.

Chapters XXI and XXII underscore the importance of appearing honorable and wise. This goal can be achieved partly through the selection of a loyal and competent personal staff. Machiavelli distinguishes between a virtuous appearance and an honorable, wise appearance. Appearing virtuous—generous, benevolent, and pious—is desirable but not necessary. However, appearing honorable and sagacious is crucial. Machiavelli's preference for some good qualities over others—for example, courage and decisiveness over generosity—is grounded in a practical argument. Generosity is undesirable because it wastes capital resources; decisiveness is desirable because it breeds respect among allies and subjects.

SUMMARY & ANALYSIS

Chapter XXIII states that, ultimately, a prince must possess independent intellect in order to succeed. He cannot simply rely on the wisdom of his advisers. In a way, this idea supports Machiavelli's allusion to the possibility that a common man can become a prince through the study of warcraft and through practical experience. Machiavelli's view of politics is more meritocratic than aristocratic, as he suggests that hereditary princes have even more to prove than those who obtain power through intelligence and skill.

Chapters XXIV–XXVI

Summary — Chapter XXIV: Why the Princes of Italy Have Lost Their States

Machiavelli suggests that any new prince who successfully follows the advice found in *The Prince* will enjoy the stability of a hereditary prince, since men are more aware of the present than of the past.

A number of Italian princes have lost states through their own military faults. They fled when they should have fought, expecting their subjects to call them back. These princes failed because of their own incompetence and not as a result of a string of bad luck. They took too much comfort in prosperous times, never anticipating danger. When they were conquered, they hoped that the people would revolt and recall them; but it is always folly to depend upon others for security. A prince's best defense is his own valor.

Summary — Chapter XXV: Concerning the Influence of Fortune in Human Affairs, and the Manner in Which It Is to Be Resisted

Although it is often thought that fortune controls human affairs, fortune controls only half of one's actions, while free will determines the other half. Fortune is like a flooding river: it is only dangerous when men have not built dykes against it beforehand. Italy has not built dykes, and as a result it has experienced tumultuous upheaval. Germany, Spain, and France have taken better care and have reaped the benefits of stability.

As fortune varies, one man may succeed and another fail, even if they both follow the same path. Times and circumstances change, so a prince must adjust to them in order to remain successful; however, men tend to stay on the course that has brought them success in the past. Circumstances allowed Julius II to act impetuously, but if he had lived longer, he would have been ruined when circumstances changed. On the whole, however, impetuosity surpasses caution. Fortune favors energetic youth over cautious age.

SUMMARY — CHAPTER XXVI: AN EXHORTATION TO FREE ITALY FROM THE HANDS OF THE BARBARIANS

Italy's current disarray favors the emergence of a new prince who will bring happiness to the Italian people. Until recently, there had been a prince who seemed ordained by heaven to redeem Italy. But a string of bad luck has prevented such an outcome.

Lorenzo de' Medici is Italy's best hope. If he has learned from the great men named in *The Prince*, the salvation of Italy will not be difficult. For though those men were great, they were still only men, with no greater opportunities or grace than Lorenzo's own. Past wars and princes have failed to strengthen Italy because its military system was old and defective.

To succeed, Lorenzo must create a national army. The Italian people are good fighters; only their leaders have failed. Lorenzo's army needs both good cavalry and infantry to defeat the Spaniards and the Swiss.

Should a prince ever succeed in redeeming Italy, he would receive unending glory and be embraced in all the provinces with love.

ANALYSIS — CHAPTERS XXIV–XXVI

Chapter XXV discusses the role of fortune in the determination of human affairs. Many thinkers have considered the question of whether a man's actions are a manifestation of his own free will, or if they are simply determined by fate or his environment. Machiavelli attempts to compromise between free will and determinism by arguing that fortune controls half of human actions and leaves the other half to free will. But Machiavelli also argues that, through foresight—a quality whose importance Machiavelli stresses throughout *The Prince*—people can shield themselves against fortune's slings and arrows. Thus, Machiavelli can be described as confident in the capabilities of human beings to shape their destinies, but skeptical that such control is absolute.

Machiavelli ends *The Prince* with an impassioned plea to redeem Italy. Stylistically, he abandons his detached tone and utilizes exhortation and poetry to communicate nationalistic fervor. He implores Lorenzo, to whom the book is dedicated, to deliver Italy. Despite Machiavelli's efforts, the country would not be truly unified for another three and a half centuries. Some have argued that *The Prince* is really the manifestation of Machievelli's desire to see a strengthened Italy, not a detached work of political science. Historical references to Italy dominate the book, and Machiavelli clearly conceives the book as a means to expedite the successful unification of Italy. But *The Prince*'s clear application to Machiavelli's home country does not distract from the book's relevance to philosophical questions. At the very least, it must be said that the book's influence spread further than the specific audience to which it was addressed.

A desire to strengthen Italy might also serve as Machiavelli's ethical justification for the advice he has given. Machiavelli has previously argued that a prince cannot achieve success without sometimes resorting to ruthlessness. But Machiavelli never justifies the obtainment of political success as a worthwhile goal in itself. His concern with Italy would justify his logic: if the ultimate end is the glory of Italy, the end would justify the means.

The Prince is full of historical references, but the final chapters place the book in a historical context. Moreover, these chapters give us some insight into the mind of the author and his motives for writing the book. They suggest that Machiavelli is not as diabolical as he is often portrayed.

SUMMARY & ANALYSIS

IMPORTANT QUOTATIONS EXPLAINED

1. At this point one may note that men must be either pampered or annihilated. They avenge light offenses; they cannot avenge severe ones; hence, the harm one does to a man must be such as to obviate any fear of revenge.

This passage from Chapter III is an example of logical reasoning conspicuously devoid of ethical considerations. A prince must realize that he has two options: benevolence and destruction. Because the latter option will cause resentment among the people, he should choose it only if he is absolutely sure there will be no ill consequences—that the destruction he incurs will eliminate or disable any parties that might seek to revenge themselves against him. Feelings of pity or compassion are meaningless. Self-interest and self-protection are in this case the motivating factors and are to be pursued ruthlessly.

2. [P]eople are by nature changeable. It is easy to persuade them about some particular matter, but it is hard to hold them to that persuasion. Hence it is necessary to provide that when they no longer believe, they can be forced to believe.

This passage from Chapter VI is an example of Machiavelli's use of assumptions about human nature to justify political action. This quotation follows a formula used throughout *The Prince*: because people are X, a prince must always do Y. Whereas Machiavelli laces his historical points with a wealth of evidence and detail, he tends not to provide significant explanations for many broad statements he makes about human nature. We may assume that when Machiavelli writes a statement such as "people are by nature changeable," he is uttering a belief generally accepted in sixteenth-century Florentine society.

3.   A prince must have no other objective, no other thought,
     nor take up any profession but that of war, its methods
     and its discipline, for that is the only art expected of a
     ruler. And it is of such great value that it not only keeps
     hereditary princes in power, but often raises men of lowly
     condition to that rank.

This quote from Chapter XIV highlights warcraft as both an aca-
demic discipline that can be studied through historical examples
and as a matter of practical experience. For Machiavelli, all affairs of government are viewed through a military lens, because
the ultimate goal of a government is self-preservation; military defense—embracing ideas of strategy, diplomacy, and geography—is
the means by which governments preserve themselves. Machiavelli
does not conceive of the prince as a man skilled in many disciplines,
but rather as one whose sole responsibility is to ensure the stability
of the state that he governs.

4.   Only the expenditure of one's own resources is harmful;
     and, indeed, nothing feeds upon itself as liberality does.
     The more it is indulged, the fewer are the means to indulge
     it further. As a consequence, a prince becomes poor and
     contemptible or, to escape poverty, becomes rapacious and
     hateful. Of all the things he must guard against, hatred and
     contempt come first, and liberality leads to both. Therefore
     it is better to have a name for miserliness, which breeds
     disgrace without hatred, than, in pursuing a name for
     liberality, to resort to rapacity, which breeds both disgrace
     and hatred.

This passage from Chapter XVI illustrates Machiavelli's attitude
toward virtue and statecraft. Machiavelli advises the prince to dis-
regard the principles of virtue when acting on behalf of his state. Instead, while it is desirable for a prince to act virtuously when he can,
he should never let perceptions of virtue interfere with statecraft.
Even though generosity seems admirable, it is ultimately detrimental to the state, and therefore should be avoided. A prince will never
be hated for lack of virtue, he will be hated only if he fails in his duty
to maintain the state. Virtuous action, in that it often promotes self-
sacrifice, often conflicts with that duty.

5.   Here a question arises: whether it is better to be loved than feared, or the reverse. The answer is, of course, that it would be best to be both loved and feared. But since the two rarely come together, anyone compelled to choose will find greater security in being feared than in being loved. . . . Love endures by a bond which men, being scoundrels, may break whenever it serves their advantage to do so; but fear is supported by the dread of pain, which is ever present.

This passage from Chapter XVII contains perhaps the most famous of Machiavelli's statements. Often, his argument that it is better to be feared than loved is taken at face value to suggest that *The Prince* is a handbook for dictators and tyrants. But a closer reading reveals that Machiavelli's argument is a logical extension of his assessments of human nature and virtue. In the first place, people will become disloyal if circumstances warrant. In the second, the prince's ultimate goal is to maintain the state, which requires the obedience of the people. From these two points, it follows that between benevolence and cruelty, the latter is the more reliable. Machiavelli never advocates the use of cruelty for its own sake, only in the interests of the ultimate end of statecraft.

KEY FACTS

FULL TITLE
The Prince

AUTHOR
Niccolò Machiavelli

TYPE OF WORK
Political treatise; letter; manual

LANGUAGE
Italian

TIME AND PLACE WRITTEN
Started in July 1513, finished in 1514; Florence, Italy

DATE OF FIRST PUBLICATION
1532, after Machiavelli's death; first English translation appeared in 1640.

THEMES
Statesmanship and warcraft; goodwill and hatred; free will; virtue; human nature

POLITICAL CONTEXT
The Prince was written during a time of political turbulence as a practical guide to help Lorenzo de' Medici stay in power. Lorenzo did not agree with many of Machiavelli's suggestions. The book appeared on the pope's "Index of Prohibited Books" in 1559.

STUDY QUESTIONS

1. *How does Machiavelli view human nature?*

Machiavelli differs from the many political theorists who offer conceptions of a "natural state," a presocial condition arising solely from human instinct and character. But while Machiavelli never puts forth a vision of what society would be like without civil government, he nonetheless presents a coherent, although not particularly comprehensive, vision of human nature.

Machiavelli mentions explicitly a number of traits innate among humans. People are generally self-interested, although their affections for others can be won and lost. They remain content and happy so long they avoid affliction or oppression. They might be trustworthy in prosperous times, but they can turn selfish, deceitful, and profit-driven in adverse times. They admire honor, generosity, courage, and piety in others, but most do not harbor these virtues. Ambition lies among those who have achieved some power, but most common people are satisfied with the way things are and therefore do not yearn to improve on the status quo. People will naturally feel obligated after receiving a favor or service, and this bond is usually not broken capriciously. Nevertheless, loyalties are won and lost, and goodwill is never absolute.

These statements about human nature often serve as justification for much of Machiavelli's advice to princes. For example, a prince should never trust mercenary leaders because they, like most leaders, are overly ambitious. At the same time, while many of Machiavelli's remarks on the subject seem reasonable, most are assumptions not grounded in evidence or popular notions and can easily be criticized. For example, a Hobbesian might argue that Machiavelli puts too much faith in people's ability to remain content in the absence of government force. A related issue to explore, then, might be the extent to which Machiavelli's political theory relies too heavily on any single, possibly fallacious depiction of human nature.

2. *Is Machiavelli's book "evil"? What role does virtue play in Macchiavelli's state?*

Some of the advice to rulers found in *The Prince*—most famously, the defense of cruelty toward subjects—has led to criticism that Machiavelli's book is evil or amoral. Moreover, the explicit separation of politics from ethics and metaphysics seems to indicate that there is no role for any kind of virtue in Machiavelli's state.

However, Machiavelli never advocates cruelty or other vices for their own sake. He advocates them only in the interests of safeguarding the state, which, in Machiavelli's view, is a kind of ultimate good in its own right. Nor does he advocate that virtue should be shunned for its own sake. Indeed, Machiavelli states several times that when it is in the interests of the state, a prince must strive to act virtuously. But virtue should never take precedence over the state. Thus, generosity, which might be admired by others, is actually detrimental to the future prosperity of the state. It is for this reason alone that a prince should avoid it.

Machiavelli's conception of virtue as defined in *The Prince* is not quite the same as that of classical theorists. Whereas Aristotle and others defined virtue in relation to some highest "good," Machiavelli settles for a much more simplistic definition: that which receives the praise of others. Thus, generosity is a virtue, in the Machiavellian sense, only because other people praise it.

3.   *Compare and contrast the different ways in which a*
       prince can rise to power.

According to Machiavelli, there are four main ways a prince can come into power. The first way is through prowess, meaning personal skill and ability. The second is through fortune, meaning good luck or the charity of friends. The third way is through crime, such as through a coup, conspiracy, or assassination. The fourth way is constitutional, meaning through the official support of either nobles or common people.

The most important comparison to be made is that between prowess and fortune. Obtaining a state through prowess is clearly more demanding than benefiting from simple good luck. But a prince gifted with his own prowess is possessed of a strong foundation to maintain that rule, whereas fortune is unpredictable and may lead as easily to a prince's deposition as it had to his rise. Thus, maintaining rule is much easier when a prince has used his own skill. Because the maintenance of rule is most important to Machiavelli, he concludes that prowess is a better route to become a prince.

A second comparison might be made between criminal and constitutional means of achieving power. Here, the main point of difference is not the skill and experience of the prince but popular attitudes toward the prince. A prince who comes to power through crime runs the greatest risk because he may be forced to commit some cruelty toward his subjects, endangering himself by breeding hatred and resentment among the populace. A constitutional prince, however, comes to power with the support of either the nobles or commoners, and his job consists mainly of keeping the unsupportive group satisfied with his rule.

To sum up, prowess is to be preferred over fortune because prowess leads to a more effective ruler who is likely to garner lasting glory. Constitutional princes are preferable to criminal princes not only because they are more effective, but also because a criminal prince can achieve nothing other than power. A constitutional prince can achieve both power and glory.

How to Write
Literary Analysis

The Literary Essay: A Step-by-Step Guide

When you read for pleasure, your only goal is enjoyment. You might find yourself reading to get caught up in an exciting story, to learn about an interesting time or place, or just to pass time. Maybe you're looking for inspiration, guidance, or a reflection of your own life. There are as many different, valid ways of reading a book as there are books in the world.

When you read a work of literature in an English class, however, you're being asked to read in a special way: you're being asked to perform *literary analysis*. To analyze something means to break it down into smaller parts and then examine how those parts work, both individually and together. Literary analysis involves examining all the parts of a novel, play, short story, or poem—elements such as character, setting, tone, and imagery—and thinking about how the author uses those elements to create certain effects.

A literary essay isn't a book review: you're not being asked whether or not you liked a book or whether you'd recommend it to another reader. A literary essay also isn't like the kind of book report you wrote when you were younger, where your teacher wanted you to summarize the book's action. A high school- or college-level literary essay asks, "How does this piece of literature actually work?" "How does it do what it does?" and, "Why might the author have made the choices he or she did?"

The Seven Steps
No one is born knowing how to analyze literature; it's a skill you learn and a process you can master. As you gain more practice with this kind of thinking and writing, you'll be able to craft a method that works best for you. But until then, here are seven basic steps to writing a well-constructed literary essay:

1. *Ask questions*
2. *Collect evidence*
3. *Construct a thesis*

4. Develop and organize arguments
5. Write the introduction
6. Write the body paragraphs
7. Write the conclusion

1. ASK QUESTIONS

When you're assigned a literary essay in class, your teacher will often provide you with a list of writing prompts. Lucky you! Now all you have to do is choose one. Do yourself a favor and pick a topic that interests you. You'll have a much better (not to mention easier) time if you start off with something you enjoy thinking about. If you are asked to come up with a topic by yourself, though, you might start to feel a little panicked. Maybe you have too many ideas—or none at all. Don't worry. Take a deep breath and start by asking yourself these questions:

- **What struck you?** Did a particular image, line, or scene linger in your mind for a long time? If it fascinated you, chances are you can draw on it to write a fascinating essay.

- **What confused you?** Maybe you were surprised to see a character act in a certain way, or maybe you didn't understand why the book ended the way it did. Confusing moments in a work of literature are like a loose thread in a sweater: if you pull on it, you can unravel the entire thing. Ask yourself why the author chose to write about that character or scene the way he or she did and you might tap into some important insights about the work as a whole.

- **Did you notice any patterns?** Is there a phrase that the main character uses constantly or an image that repeats throughout the book? If you can figure out how that pattern weaves through the work and what the significance of that pattern is, you've almost got your entire essay mapped out.

- **Did you notice any contradictions or ironies?** Great works of literature are complex; great literary essays recognize and explain those complexities. Maybe the title (*Happy Days*) totally disagrees with the book's subject matter (hungry orphans dying in the woods). Maybe the main character acts one way around his family and a completely different way around his friends and associates. If you can find a way to explain a work's contradictory elements, you've got the seeds of a great essay.

At this point, you don't need to know exactly what you're going to say about your topic; you just need a place to begin your exploration. You can help direct your reading and brainstorming by formulating your topic as a *question,* which you'll then try to answer in your essay. The best questions invite critical debates and discussions, not just a rehashing of the summary. Remember, you're looking for something you can *prove or argue* based on evidence you find in the text. Finally, remember to keep the scope of your question in mind: is this a topic you can adequately address within the word or page limit you've been given? Conversely, is this a topic big enough to fill the required length?

GOOD QUESTIONS

> *"Are Romeo and Juliet's parents responsible for the deaths of their children?"*
>
> *"Why do pigs keep showing up in* LORD OF THE FLIES?*"*
> *"Are Dr. Frankenstein and his monster alike? How?"*

BAD QUESTIONS

> *"What happens to Scout in* TO KILL A MOCKINGBIRD?*"*
> *"What do the other characters in* JULIUS CAESAR *think about Caesar?"*
> *"How does Hester Prynne in* THE SCARLET LETTER *remind me of my sister?"*

---

2. COLLECT EVIDENCE

Once you know what question you want to answer, it's time to scour the book for things that will help you answer the question. Don't worry if you don't know what you want to say yet—right now you're just collecting ideas and material and letting it all percolate. Keep track of passages, symbols, images, or scenes that deal with your topic. Eventually, you'll start making connections between these examples and your thesis will emerge.

Here's a brief summary of the various parts that compose each and every work of literature. These are the elements that you will analyze in your essay, and which you will offer as evidence to support your arguments. For more on the parts of literary works, see the Glossary of Literary Terms at the end of this section.

LITERARY ANALYSIS

ELEMENTS OF STORY   These are the *what*s of the work—what happens, where it happens, and to whom it happens.

- **Plot:** All of the events and actions of the work.
- **Character:** The people who act and are acted upon in a literary work. The main character of a work is known as the *protagonist*.
- **Conflict:** The central tension in the work. In most cases, the protagonist wants something, while opposing forces (antagonists) hinder the protagonist's progress.
- **Setting:** When and where the work takes place. Elements of setting include location, time period, time of day, weather, social atmosphere, and economic conditions.
- **Narrator:** The person telling the story. The narrator may straightforwardly report what happens, convey the subjective opinions and perceptions of one or more characters, or provide commentary and opinion in his or her own voice.
- **Themes:** The main idea or message of the work—usually an abstract idea about people, society, or life in general. A work may have many themes, which may be in tension with one another.

ELEMENTS OF STYLE   These are the *how*s—how the characters speak, how the story is constructed, and how language is used throughout the work.

- **Structure and organization:** How the parts of the work are assembled. Some novels are narrated in a linear, chronological fashion, while others skip around in time. Some plays follow a traditional three- or five-act structure, while others are a series of loosely connected scenes. Some authors deliberately leave gaps in their works, leaving readers to puzzle out the missing information. A work's structure and organization can tell you a lot about the kind of message it wants to convey.
- **Point of view:** The perspective from which a story is told. In *first-person point of view*, the narrator involves him or herself in the story. ("I went to the store"; "We watched in horror as the bird slammed into the window.") A first-person narrator is usually the protagonist of the work, but not always. In *third-person point of view*, the narrator does not participate

in the story. A third-person narrator may closely follow a specific character, recounting that individual character's thoughts or experiences, or it may be what we call an *omniscient* narrator. Omniscient narrators see and know all: they can witness any event in any time or place and are privy to the inner thoughts and feelings of all characters. Remember that the narrator and the author are not the same thing!

- **Diction:** Word choice. Whether a character uses dry, clinical language or flowery prose with lots of exclamation points can tell you a lot about his or her attitude and personality.

- **Syntax:** Word order and sentence construction. Syntax is a crucial part of establishing an author's narrative voice. Ernest Hemingway, for example, is known for writing in very short, straightforward sentences, while James Joyce characteristically wrote in long, incredibly complicated lines.

- **Tone:** The mood or feeling of the text. Diction and syntax often contribute to the tone of a work. A novel written in short, clipped sentences that use small, simple words might feel brusque, cold, or matter-of-fact.

- **Imagery:** Language that appeals to the senses, representing things that can be seen, smelled, heard, tasted, or touched.

- **Figurative language:** Language that is not meant to be interpreted literally. The most common types of figurative language are *metaphors* and *similes,* which compare two unlike things in order to suggest a similarity between them— for example, "All the world's a stage," or "The moon is like a ball of green cheese." (Metaphors say one thing *is* another thing; similes claim that one thing is *like* another thing.)

LITERARY ANALYSIS

---

3. CONSTRUCT A THESIS

When you've examined all the evidence you've collected and know how you want to answer the question, it's time to write your thesis statement. A *thesis* is a claim about a work of literature that needs to be supported by evidence and arguments. The thesis statement is the heart of the literary essay, and the bulk of your paper will be spent trying to prove this claim. A good thesis will be:

- **Arguable.** "*The Great Gatsby* describes New York society in the 1920s" isn't a thesis—it's a fact.

- **Provable through textual evidence**. "*Hamlet* is a confusing but ultimately very well-written play" is a weak thesis because it offers the writer's personal opinion about the book. Yes, it's arguable, but it's not a claim that can be proved or supported with examples taken from the play itself.

- **Surprising**. "Both George and Lenny change a great deal in *Of Mice and Men*" is a weak thesis because it's obvious. A really strong thesis will argue for a reading of the text that is not immediately apparent.

- **Specific.** "Dr. Frankenstein's monster tells us a lot about the human condition" is *almost* a really great thesis statement, but it's still too vague. What does the writer mean by "a lot"? *How* does the monster tell us so much about the human condition?

GOOD THESIS STATEMENTS

Question: In *Romeo and Juliet*, which is more powerful in shaping the lovers' story: fate or foolishness?

Thesis: "Though Shakespeare defines Romeo and Juliet as 'star-crossed lovers' and images of stars and planets appear throughout the play, a closer examination of that celestial imagery reveals that the stars are merely witnesses to the characters' foolish activities and not the causes themselves."

Question: How does the bell jar function as a symbol in Sylvia Plath's *The Bell Jar*?

Thesis: "A bell jar is a bell-shaped glass that has three basic uses: to hold a specimen for observation, to contain gases, and to maintain a vacuum. The bell jar appears in each of these capacities in *The Bell Jar*, Plath's semi-autobiographical novel, and each appearance marks a different stage in Esther's mental breakdown."

Question: Would Piggy in *The Lord of the Flies* make a good island leader if he were given the chance?

Thesis: "Though the intelligent, rational, and innovative Piggy has the mental characteristics of a good leader, he ultimately lacks the social skills necessary to be an effective one. Golding emphasizes this point by giving Piggy a foil in the charismatic Jack, whose magnetic personality allows him to capture and wield power effectively, if not always wisely."

4. DEVELOP AND ORGANIZE ARGUMENTS

The reasons and examples that support your thesis will form the middle paragraphs of your essay. Since you can't really write your thesis statement until you know how you'll structure your argument, you'll probably end up working on steps 3 and 4 at the same time.

There's no single method of argumentation that will work in every context. One essay prompt might ask you to compare and contrast two characters, while another asks you to trace an image through a given work of literature. These questions require different kinds of answers and therefore different kinds of arguments. Below, we'll discuss three common kinds of essay prompts and some strategies for constructing a solid, well-argued case.

TYPES OF LITERARY ESSAYS

- **Compare and contrast**

    Compare and contrast the characters of Huck and Jim in THE ADVENTURES OF HUCKLEBERRY FINN.

    Chances are you've written this kind of essay before. In an academic literary context, you'll organize your arguments the same way you would in any other class. You can either go *subject by subject* or *point by point*. In the former, you'll discuss one character first and then the second. In the latter, you'll choose several traits (attitude toward life, social status, images and metaphors associated with the character) and devote a paragraph to each. You may want to use a mix of these two approaches—for example, you may want to spend a paragraph apiece broadly sketching Huck's and Jim's personalities before transitioning into a paragraph or two that describes a few key points of comparison. This can be a highly effective strategy if you want to make a counterintuitive argument—that, despite seeming to be totally different, the two objects being compared are actually similar in a very important way (or vice versa). Remember that your essay should reveal something fresh or unexpected about the text, so think beyond the obvious parallels and differences.

- **Trace**

    Choose an image—for example, birds, knives, or eyes—and trace that image throughout MACBETH.

    Sounds pretty easy, right? All you need to do is read the play, underline every appearance of a knife in *Macbeth,* and then list them in your essay in the order they appear, right? Well, not exactly. Your teacher doesn't want a simple catalog of examples. He or she wants to see you make *connections* between those examples—that's the difference between summarizing and analyzing. In the *Macbeth* example above, think about the different contexts in which knives appear in the play and to what effect. In *Macbeth,* there are real knives and imagined knives; knives that kill and knives that simply threaten. Categorize and classify your examples to give them some order. Finally, always keep the overall effect in mind. After you choose and analyze your examples, you should come to some greater understanding about the work, as well as your chosen image, symbol, or phrase's role in developing the major themes and stylistic strategies of that work.

- **Debate**

    Is the society depicted in 1984 *good for its citizens?*

    In this kind of essay, you're being asked to debate a moral, ethical, or aesthetic issue regarding the work. You might be asked to judge a character or group of characters (*Is Caesar responsible for his own demise?*) or the work itself (*Is* JANE EYRE *a feminist novel?*). For this kind of essay, there are two important points to keep in mind. First, don't simply base your arguments on your personal feelings and reactions. Every literary essay expects you to read and analyze the work, so search for evidence in the text. What do characters in *1984* have to say about the government of Oceania? What images does Orwell use that might give you a hint about his attitude toward the government? As in any debate, you also need to make sure that you define all the necessary terms before you begin to argue your case. What does it mean to be a "good" society? What makes a novel "feminist"? You should define your terms right up front, in the first paragraph after your introduction.

    Second, remember that strong literary essays make contrary and surprising arguments. Try to think outside the box. In the *1984* example above, it seems like the obvious answer would be no, the totalitarian society depicted in Orwell's novel is *not* good for its citizens. But can you think of any arguments for the opposite side? Even if your final assertion is that the novel depicts a cruel, repressive, and therefore harmful society, acknowledging and responding to the counterargument will strengthen your overall case.

5. Write the Introduction

Your introduction sets up the entire essay. It's where you present your topic and articulate the particular issues and questions you'll be addressing. It's also where you, as the writer, introduce yourself to your readers. A persuasive literary essay immediately establishes its writer as a knowledgeable, authoritative figure.

An introduction can vary in length depending on the over-all length of the essay, but in a traditional five-paragraph essay it should be no longer than one paragraph. However long it is, your introduction needs to:

- **Provide any necessary context.** Your introduction should situate the reader and let him or her know what to expect. What book are you discussing? Which characters? What topic will you be addressing?

- **Answer the "So what?" question.** Why is this topic important, and why is your particular position on the topic noteworthy? Ideally, your introduction should pique the reader's interest by suggesting how your argument is surprising or otherwise counterintuitive. Literary essays make unexpected connections and reveal less-than-obvious truths.

- **Present your thesis.** This usually happens at or very near the end of your introduction.

- **Indicate the shape of the essay to come.** Your reader should finish reading your introduction with a good sense of the scope of your essay as well as the path you'll take toward proving your thesis. You don't need to spell out every step, but you do need to suggest the organizational pattern you'll be using.

Your introduction should not:

- **Be vague.** Beware of the two killer words in literary analysis: *interesting* and *important*. Of course the work, question, or example is interesting and important—that's why you're writing about it!

- **Open with any grandiose assertions.** Many student readers think that beginning their essays with a flamboyant statement such as, "Since the dawn of time, writers have been fascinated with the topic of free will," makes them sound important and commanding. You know what? It actually sounds pretty amateurish.

- **Wildly praise the work.** Another typical mistake student writers make is extolling the work or author. Your teacher doesn't need to be told that "Shakespeare is perhaps the greatest writer in the English language." You can mention a work's reputation in passing—by referring to *The Adventures of Huckleberry Finn* as "Mark Twain's enduring classic," for example—but don't make a point of bringing it up unless that reputation is key to your argument.

- **Go off-topic.** Keep your introduction streamlined and to the point. Don't feel the need to throw in all kinds of bells and whistles in order to impress your reader—just get to the point as quickly as you can, without skimping on any of the required steps.

---

6. WRITE THE BODY PARAGRAPHS

Once you've written your introduction, you'll take the arguments you developed in step 4 and turn them into your body paragraphs. The organization of this middle section of your essay will largely be determined by the argumentative strategy you use, but no matter how you arrange your thoughts, your body paragraphs need to do the following:

- **Begin with a strong topic sentence.** Topic sentences are like signs on a highway: they tell the reader where they are and where they're going. A good topic sentence not only alerts readers to what issue will be discussed in the following paragraph but also gives them a sense of what argument will be made *about* that issue. "Rumor and gossip play an important role in *The Crucible*" isn't a strong topic sentence because it doesn't tell us very much. "The community's constant gossiping creates an environment that allows false accusations to flourish" is a much stronger topic sentence— it not only tells us *what* the paragraph will discuss (gossip) but *how* the paragraph will discuss the topic (by showing how gossip creates a set of conditions that leads to the play's climactic action).

- **Fully and completely develop a single thought.** Don't skip around in your paragraph or try to stuff in too much material. Body paragraphs are like bricks: each individual one needs to be strong and sturdy or the entire structure will collapse. Make sure you have really proven your point before moving on to the next one.

- **Use transitions effectively.** Good literary essay writers know that each paragraph must be clearly and strongly linked to the material around it. Think of each paragraph as a response to the one that precedes it. Use transition words and phrases such as *however, similarly, on the contrary, therefore,* and *furthermore* to indicate what kind of response you're making.

---

7. WRITE THE CONCLUSION

Just as you used the introduction to ground your readers in the topic before providing your thesis, you'll use the conclusion to quickly summarize the specifics learned thus far and then hint at the broader implications of your topic. A good conclusion will:

- **Do more than simply restate the thesis.** If your thesis argued that *The Catcher in the Rye* can be read as a Christian allegory, don't simply end your essay by saying, "And that is why *The Catcher in the Rye* can be read as a Christian allegory." If you've constructed your arguments well, this kind of statement will just be redundant.

- **Synthesize the arguments, not summarize them.** Similarly, don't repeat the details of your body paragraphs in your conclusion. The reader has already read your essay, and chances are it's not so long that they've forgotten all your points by now.

- **Revisit the "So what?" question.** In your introduction, you made a case for why your topic and position are important. You should close your essay with the same sort of gesture. What do your readers know now that they didn't know before? How will that knowledge help them better appreciate or understand the work overall?

- **Move from the specific to the general.** Your essay has most likely treated a very specific element of the work—a single character, a small set of images, or a particular passage. In your conclusion, try to show how this narrow discussion has wider implications for the work overall. If your essay on *To Kill a Mockingbird* focused on the character of Boo Radley, for example, you might want to include a bit in your conclusion about how he fits into the novel's larger message about childhood, innocence, or family life.

- **Stay relevant.** Your conclusion should suggest new directions of thought, but it shouldn't be treated as an opportunity to pad your essay with all the extra, interesting ideas you came up with during your brainstorming sessions but couldn't fit into the essay proper. Don't attempt to stuff in unrelated queries or too many abstract thoughts.

- **Avoid making overblown closing statements.** A conclusion should open up your highly specific, focused discussion, but it should do so without drawing a sweeping lesson about life or human nature. Making such observations may be part of the point of reading, but it's almost always a mistake in essays, where these observations tend to sound overly dramatic or simply silly.

A+ Essay Checklist

Congratulations! If you've followed all the steps we've outlined above, you should have a solid literary essay to show for all your efforts. What if you've got your sights set on an A+? To write the kind of superlative essay that will be rewarded with a perfect grade, keep the following rubric in mind. These are the qualities that teachers expect to see in a truly A+ essay. How does yours stack up?

✓ Demonstrates a thorough understanding of the book

✓ Presents an original, compelling argument

✓ Thoughtfully analyzes the text's formal elements

✓ Uses appropriate and insightful examples

✓ Structures ideas in a logical and progressive order

✓ Demonstrates a mastery of sentence construction, transitions, grammar, spelling, and word choice

Suggested Essay Topics

1. *What are Machiavelli's views regarding free will? Can historical events be shaped by individuals, or are they the consequence of fortune and circumstance?*

2. *In* Discourses on Livy *(1517), Machiavelli argues that the purpose of politics is to promote a "common good." How does this statement relate to the ideas Machiavelli presents in* The Prince*?*

3. *Do you agree with Machiavelli's thesis that stability and power are the only qualities that matter in the evaluation of governments? If not, what else matters?*

4. *Discuss class conflict in* The Prince *and its relationship to successful government.*

5. *Discuss* The Prince*'s historical context. In what ways do the arguments and examples of the* The Prince *reflect that context?*

6. *Discuss the form, tone, and rhetoric of* The Prince*. Does Machiavelli's choice in this area lead to a persuasive argument? Why or why not?*

7. *How much of* The Prince *is relevant to contemporary society in an age when monarchies no longer are the primary form of government?*

A+ Student Essay

What is the role of the lion and fox in *The Prince*?

When he writes that a ruler must emulate the lion and the fox, Machiavelli means that great leaders are willing to use both force and cunning to get what they want. Throughout his tract, Machiavelli alternates between advocating a leonine and a fox-like style of leadership. He urges rulers to act with the ferocity and determination of a lion, yet he also encourages rulers to take a more thoughtful, flexible approach to statecraft. By introducing the metaphor of the lion and the fox, Machiavelli makes concrete an idea that appears and reappears throughout his writing: Successful princes are both decisive warriors and subtle thinkers.

The lion/fox pairing reminds us that politicians should possess equal measures of cleverness and brute strength. Machiavelli presents Achilles as an ideal leader—a literary figure who was tutored by Chiron the Centaur and so ruled with the intelligence of a man and the instincts of a beast. Like a lion, Achilles could get past the "wolves" he encountered on the battlefield, but like a fox, he could also get past the subtler snares of rival politicians. Lions are associated with nobility and straightforwardness, but Machiavelli points out that an effective governor must occasionally lie and commit sins of omission. Like Pope Alexander VI, great men will deceive their followers if the deception is in the followers' best interests. Thus, Machiavelli's prince combines boldness and sly wordplay, force and diplomacy.

The rest of *The Prince* builds on the opposing images of the lion and the fox. Repeatedly, Machiavelli encourages princes to mimic the uncomplicated resolve of a lion. When taking over a new principality, a prince should simply kill the existing royal family—without trying to win the family's favor, strip them of their power, or send them into exile. A strong prince should not attempt to use words to restore order to a scene of international chaos; instead, he should immediately declare war. If pressed, a prince should choose impetuousness over caution, for, as Machiavelli memorably writes, fortune is "a woman" who wants to be dominated. In each of these cases, shocking, leonine bloodlust is Machiavelli's enthusiastic prescription.

At other times, Machiavelli counsels more cautious and clever tactics for solving political problems. It's hard to picture a lion consulting an adviser, yet Machiavelli urges princes to seek out smart, well-intentioned men who will not hesitate to offer unflattering opinions. Lions do not often cultivate friendships with their enemies, yet Machiavelli writes that a prince's best allies are those among his subjects who seem to distrust him. (Skepticism is a sign of intelligence, and a thoughtful dissident is a worthier colleague than an earnest and brainless supporter.) Lions aren't known for their duplicity, yet Machiavelli encourages rulers to make false statements; your subjects will not care if you have lied to them, as long as the lie promotes the peace and stability of your kingdom. By advocating conferences, elaborate tactical maneuvers, and dishonesty, Machiavelli endorses the habits of a fox over the habits of a lion.

The dueling images of the lion and the fox have captivated readers for centuries because they quickly illustrate the complexity of Machiavelli's politics. It isn't fully possible to be both a cunning schemer and a beast, and yet political longevity depends on both subtlety and resolve. A great prince drowns out his critics and kills his rivals; a great prince also displays humility and tolerance. The difficulties implied by the fox/lion metaphor may account for the pessimism of Machiavelli's second to last chapter, in which the great thinker admits that every man is powerless before the "violent torrents" of fortune.

LITERARY ANALYSIS

GLOSSARY OF LITERARY TERMS

ANTAGONIST
> The entity that acts to frustrate the goals of the *protagonist*. The antagonist is usually another *character* but may also be a non-human force.

ANTIHERO / ANTIHEROINE
> A *protagonist* who is not admirable or who challenges notions of what should be considered admirable.

CHARACTER
> A person, animal, or any other thing with a personality that appears in a *narrative*.

CLIMAX
> The moment of greatest intensity in a text or the major turning point in the *plot*.

CONFLICT
> The central struggle that moves the *plot* forward. The conflict can be the *protagonist*'s struggle against fate, nature, society, or another person.

FIRST-PERSON POINT OF VIEW
> A literary style in which the *narrator* tells the story from his or her own *point of view* and refers to himself or herself as "I." The narrator may be an active participant in the story or just an observer.

HERO / HEROINE
> The principal *character* in a literary work or *narrative*.

IMAGERY
> Language that brings to mind sense-impressions, representing things that can be seen, smelled, heard, tasted, or touched.

MOTIF
> A recurring idea, structure, contrast, or device that develops or informs the major *themes* of a work of literature.

NARRATIVE
> A story.

NARRATOR

The person (sometimes a *character*) who tells a story; the *voice* assumed by the writer. The narrator and the author of the work of literature are not the same person.

PLOT

The arrangement of the events in a story, including the sequence in which they are told, the relative emphasis they are given, and the causal connections between events.

POINT OF VIEW

The *perspective* that a *narrative* takes toward the events it describes.

PROTAGONIST

The main *character* around whom the story revolves.

SETTING

The location of a *narrative* in time and space. Setting creates mood or atmosphere.

SUBPLOT

A secondary *plot* that is of less importance to the overall story but may serve as a point of contrast or comparison to the main plot.

SYMBOL

An object, *character,* figure, or color that is used to represent an abstract idea or concept. Unlike an *emblem,* a symbol may have different meanings in different contexts.

SYNTAX

The way the words in a piece of writing are put together to form lines, phrases, or clauses; the basic structure of a piece of writing.

THEME

A fundamental and universal idea explored in a literary work.

TONE

The author's attitude toward the subject or *characters* of a story or poem or toward the reader.

VOICE

An author's individual way of using language to reflect his or her own personality and attitudes. An author communicates voice through *tone, diction,* and *syntax.*

LITERARY ANALYSIS

A NOTE ON PLAGIARISM

Plagiarism—presenting someone else's work as your own—rears its ugly head in many forms. Many students know that copying text without citing it is unacceptable. But some don't realize that even if you're not quoting directly, but instead are paraphrasing or summarizing, *it is plagiarism* unless you cite the source.

Here are the most common forms of plagiarism:

- Using an author's phrases, sentences, or paragraphs without citing the source
- Paraphrasing an author's ideas without citing the source
- Passing off another student's work as your own

How do you steer clear of plagiarism? You should *always* acknowledge all words and ideas that aren't your own by using quotation marks around verbatim text or citations like footnotes and endnotes to note another writer's ideas. For more information on how to give credit when credit is due, ask your teacher for guidance or visit www.sparknotes.com.

LITERARY ANALYSIS

Review & Resources

Quiz

1. Where was Machiavelli born?

    A. Spain
    B. France
    C. Italy
    D. Germany

2. According to Machiavelli, which of the following statements about hereditary states is not valid?

    A. Subjects naturally love the ruling family
    B. They should retain traditional institutions
    C. Their traditional institutions should be adapted to current events
    D. They are more difficult to control than new states

3. Which of the following is a course of action that should not be taken by a prince of a new principality?

    A. Change the laws and taxes
    B. Punish insurrection
    C. Destroy the family of the former prince
    D. Establish settlements

4. Which of the following is the best means of becoming a prince?

    A. Constitution
    B. Fortune
    C. Crime
    D. Prowess

5.   Which of the following arguments does Machiavelli make about the nature of men?

   A.   They are naturally deceitful
   B.   They are naturally conflict-prone
   C.   They are naturally dissatisfied
   D.   They are naturally incompetent

6.   Which of the following is true about nobles and ministers?

   A.   It is easier to take over a state run by nobles, and easier to hold onto a state run by ministers
   B.   It is harder to take over a state run by nobles, and easier to hold onto a state run by ministers
   C.   It is harder to take over a state run by ministers, and easier to hold onto a state run by nobles
   D.   It is easier to take over a state run by nobles, and easier to hold onto a state run by nobles

7.   Which of the following is a course of action that a prince should not take in order to hold states accustomed to living freely under their own laws?

   A.   Live there in person
   B.   Devastate towns and villages
   C.   Bribe local officials
   D.   Set up an oligarchy

8.   Which is of the following is true about fortune and prowess?

   A.   Acquiring a state by prowess is hard, maintaining it is easy
   B.   Acquiring a state by fortune is hard, maintaining it is easy
   C.   Acquiring a state by fortune is hard, maintaining it is hard
   D.   Acquiring a state by prowess is hard, maintaining it is hard

REVIEW & RESOURCES

9. What is Machiavelli's approach to the use of cruelty?

   A. Inflict all the cruelty at once, then never again
   B. Inflict small amounts of cruelty consistently
   C. Never inflict cruelty at all
   D. Inflict cruelty suddenly and unpredictably

10. Under what conditions are fortresses most valuable?

   A. If they prevent rebel insurrections
   B. If they prevent enemies from invading
   C. If they prevent citizens from hating the prince
   D. If they prevent mercenaries from pillaging

11. Which if the following is not true about ecclesiastical principalities?

   A. They can be possessed by a prince
   B. They are maintained by divine power
   C. They can be ruled by a prince
   D. They have happy citizens

12. Which of the following types of troops should a prince depend on?

   A. Auxiliary troops
   B. Native troops
   C. Mercenary troops
   D. Mixed troops

13. Which of the following statements about auxiliary troops is not true?

   A. They fight well
   B. They are skilled and organized
   C. Their first loyalty is to another ruler
   D. They are just as dangerous as mercenaries

14. With which of the following statements would Machiavelli not agree?

   A. The only way to lose a state is by neglecting the art of war
   B. Good armies stem from good laws
   C. Italy has been overly dependent on mercenaries
   D. Auxiliary troops are useful in prosperous times

15. Which of the following traits is most desirable in a prince?

   A. Parsimony
   B. Generosity
   C. Trustworthiness
   D. Compassion

16. Against whom might a prince be justified in using inhumane cruelty?

   A. Against rebels
   B. Against criminals
   C. Against troops
   D. Against commoners

17. To what does Machiavelli compare a prince who breaks his word to play one foreign power off another?

   A. A trap
   B. A wolf
   C. A lion
   D. A fox

18. What quality in a prince will cause the populace to despise him?

   A. Effeminacy
   B. Miserliness
   C. Stubbornness
   D. Impulsiveness

19. What is the best defense against conspiracies?

    A. Popular support
    B. Loyal ministers
    C. A strong army
    D. Foreign allies

20. Which of the following is not a means of winning honor and prestige?

    A. Embarking on military campaigns
    B. Declaring neutrality in a conflict
    C. Throwing city-wide festivals
    D. Exhibiting outstanding ability

21. What is the mark of the best kind of intellect?

    A. The ability to explain things to others
    B. The ability to understand things for themselves
    C. The ability to understand the explanations of others
    D. The ability to guess the understanding of others

22. What is Machiavelli's historical assessment of Italy's past princes?

    A. Mostly bad luck despite good ruling
    B. Mostly bad ruling combined with a little bad luck
    C. Mostly bad ruling despite good luck
    D. Mostly bad luck combined with a little bad ruling

23. Which of the following is foremost among Machiavelli's pleas to Lorenzo de' Medici?

    A. The need to rebuild Italy's military strength
    B. The need to rebuild Italy's national infrastructure
    C. The need to rebuild Italy's national pride
    D. The need to rebuild Italy's alliances with foreign powers

24. Which of the following rulers is not an example of a ruler who triumphed on the strength of their own powers?

    A. Theseus
    B. Moses
    C. Cyrus
    D. Cesare Borgia

25. Why had a number of Italian princes of Machiavelli's time recently lost their states?

    A. Malignant acts of God
    B. Plague
    C. Their own military faults
    D. The invasion of brutal Mongol hordes

ANSWER KEY

1: C; 2: D; 3: A; 4: D; 5: A; 6: A; 7: C; 8: A; 9: A; 10: C; 11: C; 12: B;
13: D; 14: B; 15: A; 16: C; 17: D; 18: A; 19: A; 20: B; 21: B; 22: B;
23: A; 24: D; 25: C

Suggestions for Further Reading

BOCK, GISELA, QUENTIN SKINNER, and MAURIZIO VIROLI, eds. *Machiavelli and Republicanism.* New York: Cambridge University Press, 1990.

BUTTERFIELD, HERBERT. *The Statecraft of Machiavelli.* New York: Collier Books, 1962.

DE GRAZIA, SEBASTIAN. *Machiavelli in Hell.* New York: Harvester Wheatsheaf, 1989.

FALCO, MARIA, ed. *Feminist Interpretations of Niccolò Machiavelli.* University Park, PA: Pennsylvania State University Press, 2004.

KING, ROSS. *Machiavelli: Philosopher of Power.* New York: Eminent Lives, 2007.

RUDOWSKI, VICTOR ANTHONY. THE PRINCE: *A Historical Critique.* New York: Twayne Publishers, 1992.

SOLL, JACOB. *Publishing* THE PRINCE: *History, Reading, and the Birth of Political Criticism.* Ann Arbor: University of Michigan Press, 2005.

VILLARI, PASQUALE. *The Life and Times of Niccolò Machiavelli.* Trans. Linda Villari. St. Clair Shores, Michigan: Scholarly Press, 1969.

REVIEW & RESOURCES

Discovery education

galeio